beautiful crochet for heads, hands, and toes

beautiful CROCHET
for heads, hands, and toes

fabulous easy-to-crochet accessories

MELODY GRIFFITHS

NEW HOLLAND

First published in 2008 by New Holland Publishers (UK) Ltd
London · Cape Town · Sydney · Auckland

Garfield House, 86-88 Edgware Road, London W2 2EA,
United Kingdom
www.newhollandpublishers.com

80 McKenzie Street, Cape Town 8001, South Africa
Unit 1, 66 Gibbes Street, Chatswood, NSW 2067, Australia
218 Lake Road, Northcote, Auckland, New Zealand

ISBN 978-1-84773-353-5

Senior Editor: Clare Sayer
Production: Marion Storz
Design: bluegumdesigners.com
Photography: Paul Bricknell
Styling: Susie Johns
Illustrations: Carrie Hill
Stitch Diagrams: Kuo Kang Chen
Pattern checking: Sue Horan
Editorial Direction: Rosemary Wilkinson

1 3 5 7 9 10 8 6 4 2

Reproduction by Pica Digital PTE Ltd, Singapore
Printed and bound by Times Offset, Malaysia

contents

introduction

I have always loved making things. But like most people, I find it particularly satisfying to create exciting things quickly and easily and this is where crochet works so well. The stitches are simple, but using different yarns and hook sizes makes them a never-ending source of inspiration.

Here I'm delighted to offer you my latest collection of accessories.

Some of them are a contemporary update on classic themes, others fun and funky, but they are all designed to be fashionable, and also straightforward, to make. And one of the nicest things about this kind of crochet is that once you have mastered the basic stitches, chain, single crochet, half double or doubles, that's all there is to it. My aim is to get the best effect in the simplest possible way, so you will also find some unusual techniques; but I promise, they won't be difficult to do. Most of the projects can be made in a couple of evenings. Or if you're looking for a quick fix, start with the flowers, they take just a few minutes. Of course, the bigger items do take longer, but they are just as easy to do.

So with five hats, six scarves, three wraps, three bags, two belts, pairs of slippers, socks, armwarmers, mitts and gloves, plus a scattering of flower motifs, I hope that there's something here for everyone.

Whatever you choose to make, these accessories will emphasize your style, add variety to everyday clothes, put the finishing touch to an outfit, or just keep you warm and cozy. Oh, and they make perfect presents, too.

This book is divided into four classic color sections: Cream, Grey, Natural and Blue. Within each section, there's a range of tones and a variety of shades, so there's something to match or to contrast, whatever your chosen color scheme. As the designs for each section developed, they began to take on different characters—soft and dreamy for the cream touched with pinks; subtle and sophisticated greys highlighted with black and silver; textured, country styles for the natural brown, and autumn leaf shades; and sassy casuals for the blues jazzed up with hot pink and turquoise.

But this is how I've seen the designs. Because they are handmade, each project can be interpreted in your personal color scheme—changing the character maybe, but making each design your very own.

Fashions may come and fashions may go, but the delight I feel in designing unusual and individual things to wear never changes. I hope that you, too, will find things here that you can make and love forever.

crochet techniques

The basics of crochet are very simple as all the stitches are built up from the easy action of using a hook to make a loop in the yarn.

Everything you need to know to make the designs in this book is right here. Most of the designs combine just a few stitches, and you'll soon discover that once you've mastered them, you can pick up the techniques of shaping, working lacy motifs, or textured patterns very quickly.

If you are a beginner, start by following the step-by-step instructions for the stitches you need to know using a spare ball of double knitting yarn and a US E4 (3.50 mm) hook.

If you know how to crochet, please don't skip this section because some of my techniques are not always traditional, and attention to detail makes all the difference with some designs.

getting started

Here's the way I like to hold the yarn and the hook. There are other techniques but to me, this is comfortable, flexible, and easy to form the stitches properly. For clarity, the slip knot diagrams show just the yarn; however, when working the first step, you may find it easier to wind the yarn around your finger rather than lie it flat.

MAKING A SLIP KNOT

This is usually the first loop on the hook. Make a loop in the yarn, leaving a tail end at least 4 in. (10 cm) long hanging down behind. Insert the hook, catch the tail end yarn close to the loop and pull a new loop through.

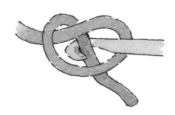

Pull gently on both ends to tighten the knot and close the loop on the hook.

HOLDING THE HOOK

I think that the easiest hooks to work with are those with a flattened area nearly half way down the shaft or hooks with a handle and a thumb pad. With the hooked end on the left facing towards you, hold the hook in your right hand like a pencil, gripping it lightly between thumb and first finger.

HOLDING THE YARN AND THE WORK

Wrap the ball-end of the yarn around the little finger of your left hand, extend the middle and third fingers so the yarn lies over them and hold the base of the slip knot between the first finger and thumb. If necessary, pull on the ball-end of the yarn to tension it over your fingers. For extra control, to tighten a loose tension or if working with fine or slippery yarns, you can wrap the yarn around the middle finger as well. Each time you make a stitch, move your thumb and first finger along to grip the work ready to make the next stitch.

the stitches

Each crochet stitch starts and ends with one loop on the hook. However complicated a crochet stitch pattern may appear to be, it is made by combining the simple stitches shown here.

CHAIN STITCH

The action of making a chain stitch is the basis of all crochet stitches.

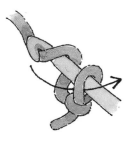

Pull a new loop through the loop on the hook. Repeat for each chain stitch.

With a slip knot on the hook, take the hook in front of the yarn and rotate the tip to take the yarn over the hook from back to front.

SLIP STITCH

Slip stitch is the shortest stitch. It's used mostly for joining stitches at the end of a round, to carry the yarn along an edge when shaping, or to get to a new place in the stitch pattern without having to break off and rejoin the yarn.

Insert hook in stitch or space as directed. Rotate tip to take the yarn over the hook from back to front, catch yarn and pull through stitch, or space and loop on hook.

working chain stitch

- Try to make your chain stitches evenly sized but not too tight. When used as a foundation for other stitches, a tight chain will pull the edge in. Ideally, your chain should be worked at the same gauge as the stitch gauge for the project. If necessary, use a larger hook, just for the starting chain.

- When counting chain, do not count the loop on the hook or the knot of the slip knot.

- There are three options when working into chain stitch. If you hold a length of chain horizontally with the chain loops at the front, you can see that each loop is divided by the next loop giving one strand at the top and one at the bottom. Turn the chain slightly and you will also see a strand at the back of each chain. If the instructions do not specify how to work into the chain stitches, insert the hook under the top and the back strand each time. Sometimes you will be directed to work into the back strand only as this gives an edge that resembles a row of single crochet. It is also possible to work into the top strand only or if working around a length of chain, into the bottom strand only.

- When working lacy patterns, chains are used to make spaces or arches between stitches. Tight chain may not stretch enough to bridge the gap. If necessary, work one or more extra chain stitches to make sure that the work lies flat.

- Chain stitch can also be used decoratively when worked on the surface of a fabric. Simply hold the yarn underneath the work and the hook above to pull the chain stitches through, moving the hook along between each stitch to create the design.

SINGLE CROCHET

Each single crochet stitch is approximately the same height and width. Single crochet can be used in rows to make a firm fabric or combined with other stitches to create stitch patterns and motifs.

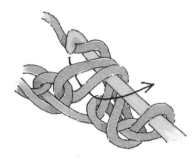

Insert hook into chain or stitch indicated in the instructions, rotate the tip of the hook to wrap the yarn around from the back to the front and pull through to make two loops on hook.

Rotate the tip of the hook to wrap the yarn around from back to front and pull through the two loops on the hook, so ending with one loop on the hook.

working single crochet

- When working into a single crochet stitch, the hook is inserted under both of the top strands of the stitch, unless otherwise directed.

- In this book, a single chain is worked at the start of each single crochet row to bring the hook up to the height of the stitches in the next row, but this chain is not worked into on the following row and it is not counted as a stitch, unless otherwise directed.

- To work a single crochet stitch around the stem of a single crochet stitch in the row below, insert the hook from the front down before the stitch designated, take it under the stitch and bring it up at the other side, wrap the yarn around the hook and pull a loop through, then wrap the yarn again and pull through the two loops on the hook.

CRAB STITCH

Crab stitch is just single crochet worked backwards. It gives a neat finish, but can make the edge flute so if necessary either skip the occasional stitch or use a smaller hook to make it lie flat.

Do not turn the work at the end of the last row. Working from left to right in the stitches along the row, insert hook in stitch, catch yarn and pull through to make two loops on hook, catch yarn and pull through two loops on hook. Repeat to end.

DOUBLE CROCHET

Double is taller than single crochet. It makes a light, flexible fabric and can be combined with other stitches to make fans, clusters, and openwork effects.

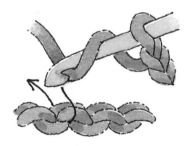

With the hook in front of the yarn, rotate the tip of the hook to wrap the yarn around from back to front. Insert hook into chain, stitch or space indicated in the instructions.

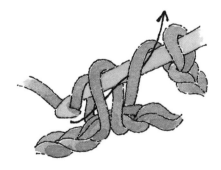

Rotate the tip of the hook to wrap the yarn around from back to front and draw the yarn through the stitch to make three loops on the hook.

Rotate the tip of the hook to wrap the yarn around from back to front and draw the yarn through the first two loops on the hook.

Rotate the tip of the hook to wrap the yarn around the hook again and draw it through the two loops on the hook.

There is now one loop on the hook and the stitch is complete.

working double crochet

- When working into a double stitch, the hook is inserted under the top two strands, unless directed otherwise.

- Traditionally, double rows start with three chain stitches to bring the yarn up to the height of the stitches in the next row. This counts as the first stitch and the first stitch of the previous row is skipped to compensate. I prefer not to do this because it leaves a gap between the first and second stitches. There are two ways of making a neater edge. Either work two chain stitches instead of three so that when the top chain is worked into on the next row, the stitches are pulled up and this closes the gap. Or, work a single crochet directly into the first stitch, then work two chain stitches. This is neat and easy because the single crochet fills the gap, the chain stitches bring you up to the height of a double and you do not need to skip any stitches.

- To work a stitch around the stem of a double, first wrap the yarn around the hook as many times as is needed for the stitch given, insert the hook from the front, down before the double stitch designated in the row below, then up after the stitch, wrap the yarn around the hook and pull a loop through, then complete the stitch in the usual way.

HALF DOUBLE

A half double is worked in the same way as a double up to the second step but instead of pulling through the first two loops, the yarn is pulled through all the loops to make a stitch that's between single crochet and double in height.

To bring the hook up to the height of a half double at the start of a row or round, work a single crochet stitch and one chain, or two chain and skip the first stitch.

TREBLE

This stitch is made in the same way as a double but with an extra step.

Wrap yarn twice around the hook, insert hook in stitch, yarn around hook and pull a loop through to give four loops on the hook, take the yarn around hook and pull through the first two loops to give three loops on hook, yarn around hook and pull through two loops to give two loops on hook, yarn around hook and pull through so ending with one loop on the hook.

To bring the hook up to the height of a treble at the start of a row or round, work a single crochet stitch and three chain or four chain and skip the first stitch.

DOUBLE TREBLE

This stitch is made in the same way as a double but with two extra steps.

Wrap yarn three times around the hook, insert hook in stitch, yarn around hook, and pull through a loop to give five loops on the hook. Take the yarn around hook and pull through the first two loops to give four loops on hook, yarn around hook and pull through two loops to give three loops on hook, yarn around hook and pull through to give two loops on hook, yarn around hook and pull through, so ending with one loop on hook.

To bring the hook up to the height of a double treble at the start of a row or round, work a single crochet stitch and four chain or five chain and skip the first stitch.

shaping and decorating

Increases and fan or shell stitch patterns are made by working two or more stitches into the same stitch or space. Decreases are made by taking two or more stitches together. Bobbles, popcorns, and puff stitches are created not only by where the stitches are placed, but also by how they are joined.

INCREASING

Working two or more complete stitches into the same stitch in the row below increases the number of stitches. When several stitches are worked into the same stitch, a fan or shell is made.

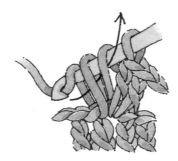

Here three double stitches are all worked into one stitch. Simply work the doubles in the usual way, but inserting the hook in the same stitch each time.

DECREASING

To join double and longer stitches together, work the first part of the stitch as usual until the last pull through. Leave the last loop of each stitch on the hook, then wrap the yarn around the hook and pull through all the loops, so joining the stitches together at the top and

leaving one loop on hook. When joining double crochet stitches, pull one loop through for each stitch, then wrap yarn around hook, and pull through all loops on hook.

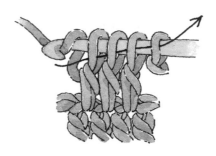

Here, three double stitches are joined together. Leaving the last loop of each stitch on the hook, work the first part of a double stitch into each of three stitches, so making four loops on the hook. Wrap the yarn around the hook and pull through all four loops to join the stitches together at the top.

BOBBLE

A bobble is made by combining increases and decreases. They can be made using three or more doubles or longer stitches.

This bobble is made with three doubles. Leaving the last loop of each stitch on the hook, work three part doubles in the same stitch so making four loops on the hook, wrap the yarn around the hook and pull through all four loops to join the stitches at the top.

POPCORN

Popcorns can be placed in a stitch or a space and are made up of any practical number of stitches.

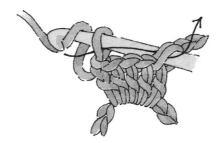

Here a five-double popcorn is worked into a chain space. Inserting hook in same place each time, work five complete doubles. Lengthen the loop on the hook slightly and slip the hook out. Insert the hook into the top of the first stitch, catch the last loop and pull it through, tightening the loop to make the popcorn stand up.

PUFF STITCH

Puff stitches are made by working part half doubles into a stitch or space, then taking the stitches together at the top. To make a puff that really stands out, gently stretch each of the first pull through loops of the half doubles to make them about the height of a double stitch.

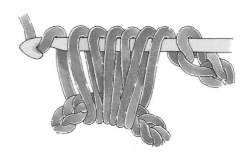

This puff stitch is made with three half doubles. To work the first part half double, wrap the yarn around the hook and insert it in a stitch or space, yarn around hook and pull a loop through, inserting hook in same stitch or space each time. Repeat this for the second and third part half doubles, so ending with seven loops on the hook. Yarn around hook and pull through all loops on hook, so ending with one loop on hook.

making a fabric

Crochet stitches can be arranged in rows or in rounds to make a flat fabric or a motif. Three-dimensional shapes can be made by working in the round.

WORKING IN ROWS

A flat fabric usually starts with a base chain. Each row of the instructions will tell you where to place the hook and which stitch to work. Simply turn the work clockwise at the end of each row. The right and the wrong side of the fabric will face you alternately.

WORKING IN ROUNDS

A tube of fabric worked in the round starts with a base chain. A motif or fabric worked in the round starts at the center with chain stitches joined in a circle or a simple ring of yarn. When working in rounds without turning, the right side of the work always faces you. If instructed to turn at the end of a round, the next round will be a wrong side round. Each round of the instructions will tell you where to place the hook and which stitches to work.

CHAIN RING CENTER

This is a very secure way of starting a motif, so it is suitable for larger projects or slippery yarn. The amount of chain needed varies with each project but 5 chain is probably the smallest size that's practical. When working into the ring, make sure that the stitches cover the chain evenly.

Make the number of chain given in the instructions, then insert hook in the first chain.

Wrap the yarn around the hook and pull a loop through both the chain and the loop on the hook.

RING OF YARN CENTER

This is a neater and less obtrusive way of starting a motif. It's quick to do and particularly good for flowers as the center can be drawn up to suit the size of the motif.

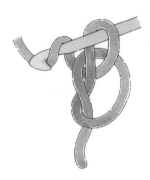

Leaving an end about 4 in. (10 cm) long hanging down, wind yarn around first finger of left hand. Insert hook in ring and catch the ball-end yarn, sliding ring of yarn off finger, pull loop through. Do not allow ring of yarn to close up or it will form a slip knot. Hold ring of yarn at the left side, moving fingers and working over tail end of yarn as you complete the first round. Just before joining the round, pull on the tail end of yarn to close the ring. Always weave this end in securely.

following the instructions

It really is a good idea to read through the instructions before starting to make a project. If there's an unfamiliar stitch or technique, try it out first before spending money on the correct yarn.

MEASUREMENTS AND MATERIALS

The measurements given are the sizes obtained using the yarn and hook size stated and working at the given gauge.

The yarn amounts are based on the quantity of yarn used to make the original item. Although the hook size given is the hook size that was used when making the original item, gauges can vary enormously in crochet so it is intended as guide only. If necessary, you can change the hook size to achieve the correct gauge.

You will also need general workbox items such as a tape measure, markers, pins, a blunt-pointed sewing needle or a tapestry needle, and scissors.

CHECKING YOUR GAUGE

Edge stitches can distort, so the best way to check your gauge is to work a few more stitches and rows than given, then to count and mark the number of stitches and rows needed. Measure between markers. If you get more than 4 in. (10 cm) your crochet is too loose, try again using a smaller hook. If you get less than 4 in. (10 cm) your work is too tight, try again using a larger hook.

Please do not skimp on this bit. Gauges in crochet seem to vary enormously, probably because the stitch size is governed equally by the gauge of the yarn in your fingers and the size of the hook. Gauge may not seem important when making a simple scarf, but if you do not match the gauge, your garment may end up much smaller or larger than the size given in the instructions, the feel of the fabric will not be the same and you may need more yarn.

UNDERSTANDING BRACKETS AND REPEATS

Where appropriate, the measurements, amount of stitches, or the amount of rows for larger sizes are given in round brackets with colons between the figures.

Instructions in square brackets should be repeated the number of times given, or repeated to the end of the row or round. Square brackets are also used to clarify working a group of stitches.

A single star * is used to indicate a repeat. Ignore the star the first time you meet it, then go back to the star and work the instructions again the number of times directed. Where there is a single star * followed later by another single star * or by two stars **, the instructions between the stars should be repeated when directed.

READING STITCH DIAGRAMS

Where appropriate, stitch patterns are also given in diagram form. The diagrams should be read in rows or in rounds in the same order as the written instructions. Each stitch is represented by a symbol placed to create a picture of the stitch pattern. Below are the basic symbols. They can be combined to show groups of stitches such as shells or popcorns.

Occasionally symbols will have been stretched or compressed for

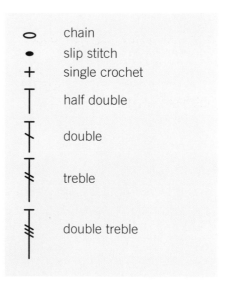

○	chain
●	slip stitch
+	single crochet
T	half double
⊤	double
⧧	treble
⧧	double treble

the sake of clarity or to fit the space. The diagrams are there to give you extra help, the written out instructions are complete without them.

COLOR CROCHET

Because the last loop of a stitch forms the top of the next stitch, when changing colors, work the last stitch in the old color until two loops remain on the hook, then use the new color to complete the stitch.

Where practical, carry the yarn not in use up at the side or inside of the work.

When necessary, cut the yarn and work over the end. When colors alternate in the same row or round, carry the yarn not in use along and slightly behind the top of the stitches in the row below and work over it until needed.

FINISHING

Many of the items in this book,

especially those worked in the round, need very little finishing, just weave in the ends and go!

Flat pieces can be sewn together or joined with crochet. If sewing, it is best to join the pieces with the right sides facing and work in the same way as joining a knitted fabric with mattress stitch, matching the rows and taking in two threads of each stitch from each side rather than whole stitches to reduce the bulk. Alternatively, you can place the right sides together and over-sew the seams. Joining a seam with crochet gives a firm, neat chain edge. This can be decorative, but can also make the seam bulky. Simply insert the hook under an edge stitch from each side and work a slipstitch or a single crochet stitch.

Whatever method you use, placing markers and pinning seams will help to match stitches or rows and give a neater finish.

crochet techniques

CROCHET HOOK SIZES

These are the most commonly used sizes.

USA	Metric	old UK
7 steel	1.50 mm	–
5 or 6	1.75 mm	15, 2$\frac{1}{2}$ or 3
1 or B	2.00 mm	14, 1$\frac{1}{2}$ or 1
2 or C	2.50 mm	12, 0 or 2/0
3 or D	3.00 mm	10, 11 or 3/0
4 or E	3.50 mm	9
5 or F	4.00 mm	8
6 or G	4.50 mm	7
8 or H	5.00 mm	6
9 or I	5.50 mm	5
10 or J	6.00 mm	4
–	6.50 mm	3
10$\frac{1}{2}$ or K	7.00 mm	2
11	7.50 mm	1
12	8.00 mm	0
15	9.00 mm	000

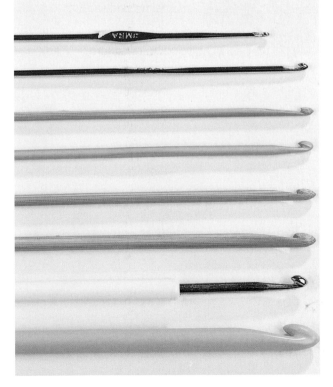

ABBREVIATIONS

ch =	chain
cont =	continue
dc =	double crochet
dec =	decrease
dtr =	double treble
foll =	following
hdc =	half double
inc =	increase
patt =	pattern
rep =	repeat
RS =	right side
sc =	single crochet
sp(s) =	space(s)
ss =	slip st
st(s) =	stitch(es)
tog =	together
tr =	treble
WS =	wrong side
yrh =	yarn around hook
[ ] =	work instructions in square brackets as directed.

crochet techniques

crochet flowers

Flowers are a natural for crochet and throughout this book, you'll find them used as decoration or as part of a motif. Here's a quick run through of the different flowers plus a few variations so you'll understand how they're constructed, leaving you free to add more flowers, to change the flowers used to decorate a project, or to use them however you want. Work your way through a few of these examples, play around with different types of yarn, and vary the amount of petals to create your own flower designs.

ABOUT THESE FLOWERS

All these flowers start with a ring in the center. Winding the yarn around your finger to make the ring allows you to ease it to the size that fits the petals when you tighten the ring by pulling on the end.

Most of these flowers have a round of single crochet worked into the ring; the amount of stitches determines the amount of petals.

All of these flowers have a chain space in the petals so you can join them to make a motif or a fabric in the same way as the four-flower motif for the fingerless gloves.

The special way of working the slip stitch between petals makes the petals curvier and more defined.

Other flowers shown here are variations on the ones used for the projects.

FOUR-PETAL FLOWER

This is the smallest flower. It has just one round and is used to make the four-flower motif for the fingerless gloves. Because the four petals are square shaped, you could easily carry on joining motifs to make a flower fabric.

Wind yarn around finger to form a ring.

Petal round (RS): [1ch, 1sc, 1dc, 1ch, 1dc, 1sc, ss in ring] 4 times. Fasten off.

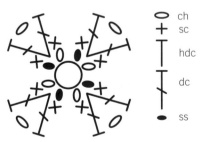

O	ch
+	sc
T	hdc
⊥	dc
●	ss

FIVE-PETAL FLOWER 1

This flower is used to decorate the beanie. It's versatile and quick to make so you can whip them up quickly and sew a bunch onto a brooch back to make a corsage, or stitch them in a line along an edge for a trimming. Although the petals have spaces, five-petal shapes don't lie flat when joined, so you could leave out the chain at the point of the petals.

Wind yarn around finger to form a ring.

1st round (RS): 1ch, 5sc in ring, pull end to close ring, remove hook, insert from front in first sc, catch loop and pull through to front.

2nd round: * [1ch, 1sc, 1hdc, 1dc, 1ch, 1dc, 1hdc, 1sc] in same sc as ss, remove hook, insert from back in same sc, catch loop and pull

through to back, remove hook, insert from front in next sc, catch loop and pull through to front, rep from * in each sc, omitting last pull through. Fasten off.

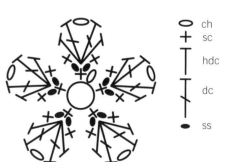

ch
sc
hdc
dc
ss

crochet techniques

FIVE-PETAL FLOWER 2

This is the flower used for the silver bag. It's made in the same way as the first five-petal flower, but with twice the amount of single crochet stitches for the center. Skipping alternate stitches between petals works well for the metallic yarn because it's not very flexible so the petals crowd together—it's a trick you could use to space out the petals whatever the type of yarn you are using or size flower you are making.

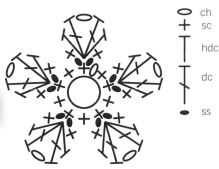

Wind yarn around finger to make a ring.

1st round (RS): 1ch, 10sc in ring, remove hook, insert from front in first sc, catch loop and pull through to front.

2nd round: * [1ch, 1sc, 1hdc, 1dc, 1ch, 1dc, 1hdc, 1sc] in first sc, remove hook, insert from back in

same sc, catch loop and pull through to back, remove hook, skip 1sc, insert hook from front in next sc, catch loop and pull through to front, rep from * 4 more times omitting last pull through to front. Fasten off.

FIVE-PETAL FLOWER VARIATIONS

For a 10-petal flower, just work one petal in each sc.

For a two-color 10-petal flower, work the first round of petals skipping alternate sc in same way as 2nd round, then join another color in a sc between petals and working 1ch when taking loop behind the existing petals to make the flower lie flatter. Make petals in each of the skipped sc.

tips

■ Always weave in the starting end thoroughly, taking it under the backs of the stitches right around the first round before snipping it off. If you prefer, you could work 4 or 5 chain and slip stitch in the first chain to form a ring. The center will be more secure, but it won't be as small.

■ The nice thing about flower motifs is that they work with whatever kind of yarn you want to use. Check the ball band to see which hook size is recommended by the manufacturer and try that size out. If you feel that your flower should be smaller or firmer, try again using a smaller hook, if you want a bigger, floppier flower, try again using a larger hook.

SIX-PETAL FLOWER

This is the flower that's scattered over the frilly mohair wrap. As well as making a lovely decoration, six-petal flowers can be joined in a hexagon pattern.

Wind yarn around finger to form a ring.

1st round (RS): 1ch, 6sc in ring, remove hook, insert from front in first sc, catch loop, and pull through to front.

2nd round: * [1ch, 1sc, 1hdc, 1dc, 1ch, 1dc, 1hdc, 1sc] in first sc, remove hook, insert from back in same sc, catch loop, and pull through to back, remove hook, insert from front in next sc, catch loop, and pull through to front, rep from * 5 times, omitting last pull through to front.

Fasten off.

○ ch
+ sc
I hdc
夫 dc
● ss

crochet techniques

If you've wondered what the flowers would look like if you just work an ordinary slip stitch between petals, look at the green six-petal flower. It's pretty, but less defined with flatter petals.

SIX-PETAL FLOWER VARIATIONS

To work a second layer of petals, join yarn at the back of one of the sc in the 1st round. Work a sc around the stem of the first sc, then keeping the yarn and hook behind the flower, work 2ch, 1sc around the stem of the next sc to the end of the round, make 2ch, ss in first sc. Starting with ss in first 2ch space, work a round of petals in the 2ch spaces.

ch — ○
sc — +
hdc — ⊤
dc — ⊤
ss — ●

cream

Soft and tender, cream is always flattering. Lift an everyday outfit with a touch of cream or lighten your mood by smothering yourself in layers of cream. For the same highlight effect in a color, opt for pearly or chalky pastel shades in pink or lilac.

aran hat

Here I've used textured crochet stitches to imitate the effect of classic Aran knitting. The hat is in one flat piece with the fat, rolled, mock-rib brim made first and the crown worked out from one edge. The diamond pattern is just double popcorns with the outline stitches worked in surface crochet afterwards.

size
Actual measurement around head 23 in. (58.5 cm)

materials
4 x 1¾ oz. (50 g) balls of Debbie Bliss Rialto DK in cream, shade 002
US F5 (4.00 mm) crochet hook
tapestry needle

gauge
20 sts and 20 rows to 4 in. (10 cm) over mock rib, 17 sts and 12 rows to 4 in. (10 cm) over patt, both using US F5 (4.00 mm) hook. Change hook size, if necessary, to obtain these gauges.

abbreviations
2dctog—leaving last loop of each st on hook, work 2dc, yrh and pull though 3 loops on hook.
3dctog—leaving last loop of each st on hook, work 3dc, yrh and pull through 4 loops on hook.
4dcpc—work 4dc in same st, remove hook, insert in first dc, catch loop and pull through to close popcorn.
See also page 17.

note
■ The brim folds back so the RS of the brim is followed by the WS of the crown.

brim
Make 31 ch.
1st row (RS): 1sc in 2nd ch from hook, [1sc in each ch] to end. 30 sts.
2nd row: 1ch, [1sc around the stem of each sc] to end.
3rd row: 1ch, [1sc in each sc] to end.
2nd and 3rd rows form mock rib patt.
Patt 98 more rows. Fasten off.

crown
With RS of brim facing, join yarn in first row-end on the right.
1st row (WS): 1ch, 2sc in same place as join, [1sc in each row-end] to end. 102 sts.
2nd row: 1ch, [1sc in each sc] to end.
3rd row: 1ch, [1sc around the stem of each sc] to end.
4th row: 1sc in first sc, 2ch, [4dcpc in next sc, 1dc in each of foll 19sc] 5 times, 1dc in last sc.
5th and every WS row: 1ch, [1sc in each st] to end.
6th row: 1sc in first sc, 2ch, [4dcpc in next sc, 1dc in each of foll 9 sc]

10 times, 1dc in last sc.
8th row: 1sc in first sc, 2ch, [4dcpc in next sc, 1dc in each of foll 7sc, 4dcpc in next sc, 1dc in each of foll 3sc, 4dcpc in next sc, 1dc in each of foll 7sc] 5 times, 1dc in last sc.
10th row: 1sc in first sc, 2ch, * 4dcpc in next sc, 1dc in each of foll 5sc, [4dcpc in next sc, 1dc in each of foll 3sc] twice, 4dcpc in next sc, 1dc in

tips

■ Save on ends when outlining bobble diamonds with surface chain by taking a 59 in. (150 cm) length of yarn and leaving 29½ in. (75 cm) at each side when joining it at the lower point of the diamond. Work the first side with one half of the yarn, then return to the other half to work the second side. Overlap the chains when weaving in the two ends at the top of the diamond.

■ If you don't outline the popcorn diamonds with surface chain and make a smaller pompom, you could get away with buying only 3 balls of yarn but the effect won't be the same.

cream

each of foll 5sc, rep from * 4 more times, 1dc in last sc.

12th row: 1sc in first sc, 2ch, [4dcpc in next sc, 2dctog, 1dc in each of foll 5sc, 4dcpc in next sc, 1dc in each of foll 3sc, 4dcpc in next sc, 1dc in each of foll 5sc, 2dctog] 5 times, 1dc in last sc. 92 sts.

14th row: 1sc in first sc, 2ch, * 4dcpc in next sc, [2dctog] twice, 1dc in each of foll 4sc, 4dcpc in next sc, 1dc in each of foll 4sc, [2dctog] twice, rep from * 4 more times, 1dc in last sc. 72 sts.

16th row: 1sc in first sc, 2ch, * 4dcpc in next sc, [2dctog] twice, 1dc in each of foll 5sc, [2dctog] twice, rep

Textured crochet stitches to imitate the effect of classic Aran knitting

ch
sc
sc around stem of st indicated by curved end of symbol

dc

4dcpc

2dctog

3dctog

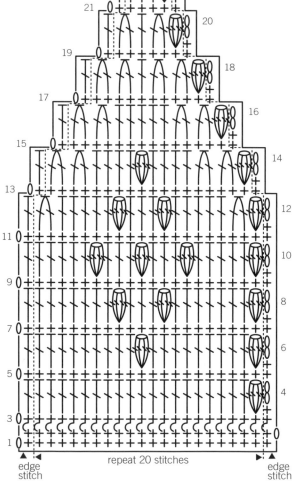

repeat 20 stitches

edge stitch

edge stitch

cream

from * 4 more times, 1dc in last sc. 52 sts.

18th row: 1sc in first sc, 2ch, *4dcpc in next sc, [2dctog] twice, 1dc in next sc, [2dctog] twice, rep from * 4 more times, 1dc in last sc. 32 sts.

20th row: 1sc in first sc, 2ch, [4dcpc in next sc, 2dctog, 1dc in foll sc, 2dctog] 5 times, 1dc in last sc. 22 sts.

22nd row: 1sc in first sc, 2ch, [4dcpc

in next sc, 3dctog] 5 times, 1dc in last sc. 12 sts.

24th row: 1sc in first sc, 2ch, [2dctog] 5 times, 1dc in last sc. 7 sts.
Fasten off.

to finish

Thread end through 7 sts of last row, draw up and secure. Using a tapestry needle and taking one st in

from each side, join back seam, reversing seam for turned back brim. Work two rows of surface chain to outline each bobble diamond. Weave in ends. Make a 2 in. (5 cm) pompom and sew on top. Fold brim back twice.

cream

rolled rose ripple brim hat

There's a traditional, simple way of making a rose by rolling a narrow strip of crochet, but, I wondered, would it be possible to make a rose be an extension of the brim of a hat and would it make the brim roll back in a pretty, flattering way? Look at this elegant hat; I think the answer is yes!

size
Actual measurement around head 21½ in. (55 cm)

materials
5 x 1¾ oz. (50 g) balls of Debbie Bliss Pure Silk in pale pink, shade 17
US C2 and US D3 (2.50 mm and 3.00 mm) crochet hooks

gauge
24 sts to 4 in. (10 cm) using US C2 (2.50 mm) hook, 23 sts and 26 rounds to 4 in. (10 cm) using US D3 (3.00 mm) hook, both over single crochet in the round. Change hook sizes, if necessary, to obtain these gauges.

abbreviations
See page 17.

notes
- The silk is worked using a smaller hook than usual for a DK weight yarn to give a firm fabric that holds its shape.

- Try the hat band on to check that it fits comfortably before continuing with the rest of the hat. If the band is too tight, work it again using a larger hook, if it is too big, work it again using a smaller hook.

band
Using US C2 (2.50 mm) hook, make 132 ch, ss in first ch to form a ring.
1st round (RS): 1ch, 1sc in same place as join, [1sc in each ch] to end, ss in first sc.
2nd round: 1ch, 1sc in same place as join, [1sc in each sc] to end, ss in first sc. 2nd round forms sc.
Work 3 more rounds.

crown
Change to US D3 (3.00 mm) hook.

shape outwards
1st round (RS): 1ch, [1sc in each of next 10sc, 2sc in foll sc] 12 times, ss in first sc. 144 sts.
2nd round: 1ch, [1sc in each of next 11sc, 2sc in foll sc] 12 times, ss in first sc. 156 sts.
3rd round: 1ch, [1sc in each of next 12sc, 2sc in foll sc] 12 times, ss in first sc. 168 sts.
4th round: 1ch, [1sc in each of next 13sc, 2sc in foll sc] 12 times, ss in first sc. 180 sts.
5th round: 1ch, [1sc in each of next 14sc, 2sc in foll sc] 12 times, ss in first sc. 192 sts.
6th round: 1ch, [1sc in each of next 15sc, 2sc in foll sc] 12 times, ss in first sc. 204 sts.
7th round: 1ch, [1sc in each of next 16sc, 2sc in foll sc] 12 times, ss in first sc. 216 sts.
Work 15 rounds sc.

shape top
1st round: 1ch, [1sc in each of next 17sc, skip 1sc] 12 times, ss in first sc. 204 sts.
Work 3 rounds sc.
5th round: 1ch, [1sc in each of next 16sc, skip 1sc] 12 times, ss in first sc. 192 sts.
Work 3 rounds sc.
9th round: 1ch, [1sc in each of next 15sc, skip 1sc] 12 times, ss in first sc. 180 sts.
Work 3 rounds sc.
13th round: 1ch, [1sc in each of next 14sc, skip 1sc] 12 times, ss in first sc. 168 sts.
Work 1 round sc.
15th round: 1ch, [1sc in each of next 13sc, skip 1sc] 12 times, ss in first sc. 156 sts.

cream

*The rolled rose
is part of the
brim of the hat*

Work 1 round sc.

17th round: 1ch, [1sc in each of next 12sc, skip 1sc] 12 times, ss in first sc. 144 sts.

Work 1 round sc.

19th round: 1ch, [1sc in each of next 11sc, skip 1sc] 12 times, ss in first sc. 132 sts.

Work 1 round sc.

21st round: 1ch, [1sc in each of next 10sc, skip 1sc] 12 times, ss in first sc. 120 sts.

Work 1 round sc.

23rd round: 1ch, [1sc in each of next 9sc, skip 1sc] 12 times, ss in first sc. 108 sts.

Work 1 round sc.

25th round: 1ch, [1sc in each of next 8sc, skip 1sc] 12 times, ss in first sc. 96 sts.

Work 1 round sc.

27th round: 1ch, [1sc in each of next 7sc, skip 1sc] 12 times, ss in first sc. 84 sts.

Work 1 round sc.

29th round: 1ch, [1sc in each of next 6sc, skip 1sc] 12 times, ss in first sc. 72 sts.

Work 1 round sc.

31st round: 1ch, [1sc in each of next 5sc, skip 1sc] 12 times, ss in first sc. 60 sts.

Work 1 round sc.

33rd round: 1ch, [1sc in each of next 4sc, skip 1sc] 12 times, ss in first sc. 48 sts.

Work 1 round sc.

35th round: 1ch, [1sc in each of next 3sc, skip 1sc] 12 times, ss in first sc. 36 sts.

Work 1 round sc.

37th round: 1ch, [1sc in each of next 2sc, skip 1sc] 12 times, ss in first sc. 24 sts.

Work 1 round sc.

39th round: 1ch, [1sc in next sc, skip 1sc] 12 times, ss in first sc. 12 sts.

Work 1 round sc.

41st round: 1ch, [1sc in next sc, skip 1sc] 6 times, ss in first sc. 6 sts. Fasten off. With WS facing, thread end through sts of last round, draw up and secure.

tip

■ Counting so many chain stitches for the band accurately can be tricky. There are two ways of tackling this. Make it easier to check by marking every 12th chain with a safety pin. Or, instead of joining the chain in a ring, make an extra chain in case you've miscounted, then turn and work a row of sc, counting carefully and omitting and later undoing any extra chain, join in a ring at the end of the first round, then join the chain edge when weaving in the end.

cream

brim

With RS facing and hat upside down, fold the first 3 rounds of the band down into the crown. Using US C2 (2.50 mm) hook, join yarn in first sc of 4th round.

Preparation round (RS): 1ch, 1sc in each sc of 4th round, ss in first sc. 132 sts.

Change to US D3 (3.00 mm) hook. Work 1 round sc.

shape rosette

1st round: 1ch, [1sc in each of next 10sc, 2sc in foll sc] 4 times, make 25ch, 1sc in 2nd ch from hook, 1sc in each of next 23ch, [1sc in each of next 10sc, 2sc in foll sc] 8 times, ss in first sc. 168 sts.

2nd round: 1ch, [1sc in each of next 11sc, 2sc in foll sc] 4 times, [1sc in base of each of next 11ch, 2sc in base of foll ch] twice, [1sc in each of next 11sc, 2sc in foll sc] 10 times, ss in first sc. 208 sts.

3rd round: 1ch, [1sc in each of next 12sc, 2sc in foll sc] 16 times, ss in first sc. 224 sts.

4th round: 1ch, [1sc in each of next 13sc, 2sc in foll sc] 16 times, ss in first sc. 240 sts.

5th round: 1ch, [1sc in each of next 14sc, 2sc in foll sc] 16 times, ss in first sc. 256 sts.

6th round: 1ch, [1sc in each of next 15sc, 2sc in foll sc] 16 times, ss in first sc. 272 sts.

7th round: 1ch, [1sc in each of next 16sc, 2sc in foll sc] 16 times, ss in first sc. 288 sts.

8th round: 1ch, [1sc in each of next 17sc, 2sc in foll sc] 16 times, ss in first sc. 304 sts.

9th round: 1ch, [1sc in each of next 18sc, 2sc in foll sc] 16 times, ss in first sc. 320 sts.

10th round: 1ch, [1sc in each of next 19sc, 2sc in foll sc] 16 times, ss in first sc. 336 sts.

11th round: 1ch, [1sc in

each of next 20sc, 2sc in foll sc] 16 times, ss in first sc. 352 sts.

Work 1 round sc, then work 1 round crab stitch (sc backwards).

Fasten off.

to finish

Press lightly to enhance shape. Weave in ends. Roll the rosette extension and stitch in place.

luxury scarf

This scarf uses the simplest of stitch patterns, just alternate rows of double and single crochet. Because it's made in a luxurious yarn that's a mix of extra-fine Merino wool and Angora worked on a larger than usual hook to give a soft, floppy fabric, it's really very special.

size

Actual measurements: width 10 in. (25 cm); length (excluding fringe) 60 in. (152 cm)

materials

4 x 1¾ oz. (50 g) balls of Sublime Angora Merino in Giggle, shade 0072
US J10 and US K10½ (6.00 mm and 7.00 mm) crochet hooks

gauge

13 sts and 9 rows (measured over 5 rows sc, 4 rows dc) to 4 in. (10 cm) over patt using US J10 (6.00 mm) hook. Change hook size, if necessary, to obtain this gauge.

abbreviations

See page 17.

note

■ To give a neat edge, 2 ch are worked at the beginning of each double row. These 2 ch are counted as the first stitch on a double row.

scarf

Using US K10½ (7.00 mm) hook, make 34ch.
Change to US J10 (6.00 mm) hook.
1st row: 1sc in 2nd ch from hook, [1sc in each ch] to end. 33 sts.
2nd row (RS): 2ch, skip first sc, [1dc in each sc] to end.
3rd row: 1ch, 1sc in each dc, 1sc in 2nd ch.
2nd and 3rd rows form the patt. Patt 134 more rows, so ending with a row of sc. Do not fasten off, turn.
1st fringe row: Make 11ch, ss in 2nd ch from hook, ss in each of next 9ch, * working in top strand only of each st, ss in each of next 2sc, 11ch, ss in 2nd ch from hook, ss in each of next 9ch, rep from * to end. Fasten off.
2nd fringe row: Using US J10 (6.00 mm) hook and with same side of scarf as first fringe row facing, join yarn in base of first ch at the start of the scarf and working in base of ch instead of sc, complete as 1st fringe row.

tips

■ Weave in the ends as you work and your scarf is ready to wear.

■ It's easier to hide the ends if you join in new yarn a few stitches in from the edge.

cream

skinny sleeves wrap

When is a wrap not a wrap? When it's a jacket! This versatile garment contrasts lacy motifs that can be quickly worked in odd moments with bands of single crochet for structure and stability. The sleeves are superlong and very close fitting, but that's the only bit that fits. How you wear the rest is up to you— wrap, tie, or leave the ends to drift and float.

size

One size, with different sleeve sizes
Actual measurements: across back 17 in. (43 cm); across each front 25¼ in. (64 cm); total width (from right front edge to left front edge) 67¼ in. (171 cm); total length 23½ in. (60 cm); sleeves around cuff 7(8:8½:9) in. [18(20:21.5:23) cm]; sleeves around top arm 12¼(13:13¾:14½) in. [31.5(33:35:36.5) cm]; sleeve length 23½ in. (60 cm)

Figures in round brackets refer to larger sizes; one figure refers to all sizes. Choose your size by measuring your wrist and top arm and working the appropriate size sleeves.

materials

12 (13:14:15) x ⅞ oz. (25 g) balls of Sublime Kid Mohair Blend in Vellum, shade 029
US H8 (5.00 mm) crochet hook

gauge

Each flower square measures 4¼ x 4¼ in. (11 x 11 cm), 12 sts and 16 rows to 4 in. (10 cm) over sc in rows, 12 sts and 14 rows to 4 in. (10 cm) over sc in rounds all when lightly steamed, using US H8 (5.00 mm) hook. Change hook size, if necessary, to obtain this size square and these gauges.

flower square

Wind yarn around finger to form a ring.
1st round (RS): 1ch, 1sc in ring, 2ch, 15dc in ring, ss in 2nd ch.
2nd round: 1ch, [1sc, 1ch, 2dctog] in same place as ss, 4ch, [skip 1dc, 3dctog in next dc, 4ch] 7 times, skip last dc, ss in 2dctog.
3rd round: Ss in first 4ch sp, 1ch, [1sc, 1ch, 2dctog, 2ch, 3dctog] in first 4ch sp, 4ch, [3dctog, 2ch] twice in same 4ch sp, * [3dctog, 2ch] twice in next 2ch sp, [3dctog, 2ch, 3dctog, 4ch, 3dctog, 2ch, 3dctog] in foll 4ch sp, 2ch, rep from * 2 more times, [3dctog, 2ch] twice in last 4ch sp, ss in 2dctog.
Fasten off.
Make 32 flower squares.

plain bands

1st row: 4ch, 1sc in 4th ch from hook, [5ch, 1sc in 4th ch from hook] 30 times. 31 picots.
2nd row: Ss in 1st picot, 1ch, 1sc in 1st picot, [1sc over ch between picots, 1sc in next picot] 30 times. 61 sts.

3rd row: 1ch, [1sc in each sc] to end **.
3rd row forms sc.
Work 6 more rows sc.
10th row: [1sc, 3ch, 1sc] in first sc, * ss in next sc, [1sc, 3ch, 1sc] in foll sc, rep from * 29 more times.
Fasten off.
Make 5 plain bands.

sleeves

Make 22(24:26:28)ch, ss in first ch to form a ring.
1st round: 1ch, 1sc in same place as ss, [1sc in each ch] to end, ss in first sc, turn. 22(24:26:28) sts.
2nd round: 1ch, [1sc in each sc] to end, ss in first sc, turn.
2nd round forms sc.
Turning at the end of each round, work 33 more rounds sc.
Inc round (RS): 1ch, 1sc in same place as ss, 2sc in next sc, [1sc in each sc] to last sc, 2sc in last sc, ss in first sc. 24(26:28:30) sts.
Turning at the end of each round, cont in sc, inc in this way on 3 foll 4th rounds and on 4 foll 6th rounds. 38(40:42:44) sts.

abbreviations

3dctog—leaving last loop of each st on hook, work 3dc, yrh and pull though 4 loops on hook.
See also page 17.

Turning at the end of each round, work 11 more rounds sc.
Fasten off.

sleeve bands

Work as plain band to **. Work 1 more row sc.

1st joining row (RS): 1ch, 1sc in each of first 34(33:32:31)sc, 2ch, starting at end of round at underarm of sleeve, work 1sc in first sc of sleeve, [2ch, 1sc in next sc of band, 2ch, 1sc in next sc of sleeve] 18(19:20:21) times, 2ch, 1sc in each of last 9sc of band.

2nd joining row: 1ch, 1sc in each of first 9sc, 2ch, 1sc in first free sc of sleeve, [4ch, 1sc in next sc of sleeve] 18(19:20:21) times, 2ch, 1sc in each of last 34(33:32:31)sc of band.

3rd joining row: 1ch, 1sc in each of first 34(33:32:31)sc, 1sc in each of next 18(19:20:21) 4ch sps, 1sc in each of last 9sc. 61 sts.

Work 2 more rows sc, then work 10th row as given for plain band. Make and join one of these bands to each sleeve.

to finish

Join flower squares.

Joining row: Join yarn in a corner 4ch sp of 1st square, with RS of 2 squares together work 1ch, 1sc in same sp as join, 2ch, 1sc in corner sp of 2nd square, [2ch, 1sc in next sp of 1st square, 2ch, 1sc in next sp of 2nd square] 6 times. Fasten off.

Join 3rd square to 2nd square and 4th square to 3rd square in same way to make a line of 4 squares. Join remaining squares in the same way to make 7 more lines of 4 squares. Working in the same way alternately in sps and picots, join lines of squares and plain bands in order of [1 line of squares, 1 plain band] twice, 1 line of squares, right sleeve band, 1 line of squares, 1 plain band, 1 line of squares, left sleeve band, [1 line of squares, 1 plain band] twice, 1 line of squares.

edging

With WS facing, join yarn in lower left corner sp.

1st round: 1ch, * 1sc in corner sp, [3ch, 1sc] twice in same corner sp *,

tips

- If you want to make the wrap without the sleeves, you'll only need 10 x 7/8 oz. (25 g) balls of yarn. Simply omit the sleeves, make 7 plain bands, then join motifs and bands and work edging in the same way as given.

- This is an ideal project to work on the go or while travelling but it could get grubby in your bag so keep your work clean while carrying it about by storing it in a pillowcase.

- Mark the sleeve increases with contrast threads or safety pins to make it easier to count the rounds between them.

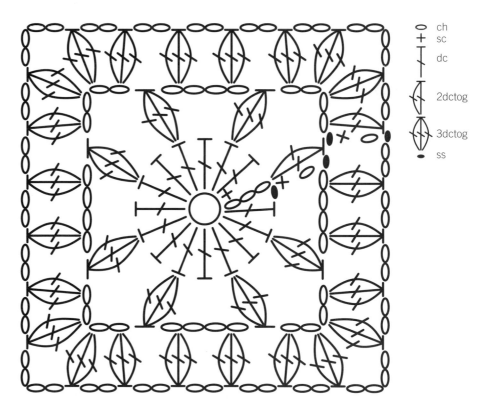

○	ch
+	sc
┬	dc
	2dctog
	3dctog
•	ss

Leave the ends to drift and float, wrap them tight across your body, or throw them over your shoulders. It's all in soft, kid mohair so whatever your style, the effect is very glamorous

[1sc, 3ch, 1sc] in each of next 30 sps up left front, rep from * to * in corner sp, [1sc, 3ch, 1sc] in each of next 8 sps **, [1sc in next row-end, 3ch, 1sc in foll row-end] 4 times ***, [1sc, 3ch, 1sc] in each of next 11 sps, rep from ** 5 times, rep from ** to ***, [1sc, 3ch, 1sc] in each of last 8 sps of upper edge, work from first * down right front edge and along lower edge, ending 1sc, 3ch in first corner sp, ss in first sc.

2nd round: Ss in first 3ch sp, 1ch, * [1sc, 3ch, 1sc] in corner 3ch sp, 2sc in each of next 31 sps, [1sc, 3ch, 1sc] in next corner 3ch sp, 2sc in each of next 112 sps, rep from * once more, ss in first sc, turn.

3rd round: 1ch, 1sc in 3ch sp, * 1sc in each of next 226sc, 1sc, 3ch, 1sc in corner sp, 1sc in each of next 64sc, 1sc, 3ch, 1sc in corner sp, rep from * once more omitting last sc, ss in first sc, turn.

4th round: 1ch, * [1sc, 3ch, 1sc in corner 3ch sp, 1sc in each of next 66sc, [1sc, 3ch, 1sc] in corner 3ch sp, 1sc in each of next 228sc, rep from * once more, ss in first sc, turn.

5th round: 1ch, 1sc in 3ch sp, * 1sc in each of next 230sc, 1sc, 3ch, 1sc in corner sp, 1sc in each of next 68sc, 1sc, 3ch, 1sc in corner sp, rep from * once more omitting last sc, ss in first sc, turn.

Picot round: 1ch, ** [1sc, 4ch, 1sc] in corner 3ch sp, * ss in next sc, [1sc, 4ch, 1sc] in foll sc *, rep from * to *

tips

- You could easily adapt this design to make a wrap entirely of flower square motifs. To make a longer or wider wrap, add extra lines of flower squares and plain bands; or add extra motifs to each line and extend the plain bands to fit, adjusting the edging to match. Remember to allow for more yarn if you are making a bigger wrap.

- Kid mohair blend should not be pressed so to finish the work neatly. You can either lightly spray the pieces with a water mister and pin them out flat to dry before making up or steam the finished garment by laying it flat, in sections depending on the size of your ironing board. Gently shooting steam over it from a steam iron, making sure that the iron never touches the surface of the crochet.

to corner, rep from ** 3 more times, ss in first sc.
Fasten off.

Finish cuff edges by joining yarn in base of first ch at lower edge of sleeves and working a picot round to match edging.
Weave in all ends.

textured bag

Super thick yarn makes this bag super quick to crochet. The stitches are so big, it's easy to see them when working the interesting textured panel and the rest of the bag is just single crochet. The bag is tough enough to carry shopping but soft enough to store your crochet projects in, so why not make two?

bag

Make 60ch, remove hook, insert under strand behind first ch, catch last ch and pull through to join ch in a ring.

1st round (WS): Working into strand behind ch each time, 1ch, [1sc in each ch] to end, ss in first sc, turn. 60 sts.

2nd round (RS): 1ch, 1sc in same place as ss, 1sc in next sc, [1dc around the stem of each of next 2sc, 1sc in each of foll 2sc] 6 times, [1sc in each sc] to end, ss in first sc, turn.

3rd and every WS round: 1ch, [1sc in each st] to end, ss in first sc, turn.

4th round: 1ch, 1sc in same place as ss, 1sc in next sc, [skip next 4sc and first 2dc in row below, 1dtr around

notes

■ The bag is worked in the round from the top down.

■ Take hook to front to work all stitches worked in stitches of row below.

the stem of each of next 2dc in row below, 1sc in each of last 2 of 4 skipped sc, 1dtr around the stem of each of 2 skipped dc in row below, skip next 2sc, 1sc in each of foll 2sc] 3 times, 1sc in each of last 34sc, ss in first sc, turn.

6th round: 1ch, 1sc in same place as ss, 1sc in next sc, 1dc around stem of each of next 2dtr in row below, [skip 2sc, 1sc in each of foll 2sc, skip 4sc and 2dtr in row below, 1dtr around the stem of next 2 dtr in row below, 1sc in each of last 2 of 4 skipped sc, taking hook under 2dtr just worked to make a lattice, work 1dtr around the stem of each of 2 skipped dtr in row below] twice, skip 2sc, 1sc in each of next 2sc, 1dc around stem of each of next 2dtr in row below, skip 2sc, 1sc in each of last 36 sc, ss in first sc, turn.

8th round: As 4th but working into dc in row below at each side and dtr in row below in repeat pattern.

10th to 16th rounds: Work 6th and 8th rounds two more times.

18th round: 1ch, 1sc in same place as ss, 1sc in next sc, [1dc around the

size

Actual measurements: circumference 32 1/2 in. (83 cm); height (from first decrease round at base to top edge) 10 in. (25 cm)

materials

6 x 3 1/2 oz. (100 g) balls of Sirdar Bigga in Cream, shade 685
US 15 (9.00 mm) crochet hook

gauge

22 sts of front panel measure 10 in. (25 cm), 6 1/2 sts and 8 rows to 4 in. (10 cm) over sc in rounds using US 15 (9.00 mm) hook. Change hook size, if necessary, to obtain this size panel and this gauge.

abbreviations

See page 17.

Super-thick yarn makes this bag really quick to crochet

stem of each of next 2dtr in row below, skip 2sc, 2sctog] 5 times, 1dc around the stem of each of last 2dtr in row below, skip 2sc, [1sc in each of next 3sc, 2sctog] 7 times, 1sc in last sc, ss in first sc, turn. 48 sts.

20th round: 1ch, 1sc in same place as ss, [2sctog, 1sc in each of next 2sc] 11 times, 2sctog, 1sc in last sc, ss in first sc, turn. 36 sts.

22nd round: 1ch, 1sc in same place as ss, [2sctog, 1sc in next sc] 11 times, 2sctog, ss in first sc, turn. 24 sts.

23rd round: 1ch, [2sctog] 12 times, ss in first 2sctog. 12 sts.
Fasten off.

handles

1st row: Make 2ch, 1sc in 2nd ch from hook, [1sc in side of previous sc] 65 times, turn. 66 sts.

2nd row: 1sc over each sc of 1st row. Fasten off. Weave in ends.
Make 2nd handle in the same way.

tips

- The handles will hide the bump made by the turn at the end of the rounds, but for a really neat finish, instead of working an ordinary ss, remove hook, then turn, insert in first sc, catch loop and pull through to join round each time.

- The bag takes almost all of the yarn so take care not to waste any.

- To join in new yarn, simply pull through the last step of whatever stitch you are working with the new yarn, then weave in the ends in opposite directions along the round.

to finish

Weave in ends. Press lightly on WS. With ends of handle at base of bag and leaving 24 sts at center free, pin first handle in place along each side of textured panel, stitch securely, and remove pins. Leaving 10sc at each side of bag, sew 2nd handle in place to match.

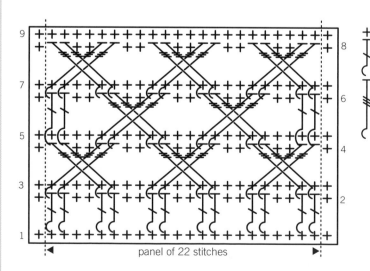

panel of 22 stitches

+ sc

dc around stem of stitch indicated by curved end of symbol

dtr around stem of stitch indicated by curved end of symbol

cream

slouchy socks

These cozy, candy-striped socks are the ultimate in comfort. Wear them in bed and around the house or with roomy slip-on clogs or boots.

size

Actual measurements: around foot 9 in. (22.5 cm); length from heel to toe 9 in. (22 cm)

materials

2 x 1³/₄ oz. (50 g) balls of Debbie Bliss Rialto DK in pale pink, shade 14 (A)
1 x 1³/₄ oz. (50 g) ball same in cream, shade 02 (B)
US J10 (6.00 mm) crochet hook

gauge

15 sts and 16 rows to 4 in. (10 cm) over single crochet in rounds using US J10 (6.00 mm) hook. Change hook size, if necessary, to obtain this gauge.

abbreviations

See page 17.

right sock

heel

Using A, make 11ch.

1st round (RS): 1sc in 4th ch from hook, 1sc in each of last 7ch, make 3ch, 1sc in base of each of 8ch already worked into.

2nd round: 3sc in first 3ch sp, 1sc in each of next 8sc, 3sc in 2nd 3ch sp, 1sc in each of last 8sc. 22 sts.

3rd round: 1sc in first sc, 3sc in next sc, 1sc in each of foll 10sc, 3sc in next sc, 1sc in each of last 9sc. 26 sts.

Work 1 round sc.

5th round: 1sc in each of first 2sc, 3sc in next sc, 1sc in each of foll 12 sc, 3 sc in next sc, 1sc in each of last 10sc. 30 sts.

Work 1 round sc.

7th round: 1sc in each of first 3sc, 3sc in next sc, 1sc in each of foll 14sc, 3sc in next sc, 1sc in each of last 11sc. 34 sts.

Work 1 round sc. Fasten off.

toe

Work as given for heel, do not fasten off, change to B at end of last round.

foot

Work in stripe patt of [2 rounds B, 2 rounds A] 4 times, 2 rounds B, 1 round A. Fasten off.

join heel

Folding along the lines of increases, flatten heel and foot. With RS together and heel towards you, matching steps at end of last round of foot and last round of heel, hold heel edge against foot edge. Using A, starting at increase side of heel

notes

■ The socks are worked in the round in a spiral from the toes upwards with the RS facing. The heel is made first so it is ready to join in after the foot has been worked.

■ To change colors neatly, work the second pull-through of the last stitch of the last round of a stripe in the next color.

cream

*These socks
are the ultimate
in comfort*

and inserting hook through one st of heel and one st of foot together each time, join 17 sts **.

top

Continue in A on remaining sts of foot and heel.

1st round (RS): Across foot, 1sc in each of first 2sc, [2sc in next sc, 1sc in each of foll 2sc] 5 times, across heel, 1sc in each sc, changing to B at end of round.
39 sts.
Cont in sc, work [2 rounds B, 2 rounds A] 5 times, then work 2 rounds B.
Cont in A, work 9 rounds sc, then work to center back and ss in next sc. Fasten off.
Weave in ends and press lightly.

left sock

As right sock to **. Fasten off. Join A in first of remaining 17 sts of heel.

1st round: Across heel, 1ch, 1sc in same sc as join, 1sc in each of next 16sc, across foot, 1sc in each of first 2sc, [2sc in next sc, 1sc in each of foll 2sc] 5 times. 39 sts.
Complete as given for right sock.

tips

- Mark the start of the rounds with a contrast thread taken between the stitches to the back and front of the work alternately.

- When working the 2 round stripes, there's no need to break off the yarn not in use, just carry it loosely over the contrast stripe on the WS.

- Because they're worked in the round, it's easy to try the socks on as you make them. If you want to adjust the length of the foot or make the top of the socks shorter or longer, omit or add 4 rounds in stripe pattern. If you make the socks longer, you'll need more yarn.

- If you want to make the socks in one color, just omit the stripe pattern. You'll still need 3 x 1¾ oz. (50 g) balls of Rialto DK.

cream

grey

Sophisticated and sharp, grey looks effortlessly elegant. Explore all the shades from subtle smoky grey through to stormy blue-grey. If you're looking for a dramatic contrast, choose deepest charcoal black or a blaze of metallic silver.

baggy beret

This versatile, textured, slouchy beret can be worn draped to one side, perched on the back of your head, or with your hair tucked in like a snood. And it's a quick make too with just twenty-one rounds in the puff stitch pattern top.

size
Actual measurement around band 22 in. (56 cm)

materials
3 x 1¾ oz. (50 g) balls of Debbie Bliss Rialto DK in pale grey-green, shade 17
US F5 (4.00 mm) crochet hook

gauge
16 sts to 4 in. (10 cm) over single crochet, 6 sts and 10 rows to 4 in. (10 cm) over puff stitch, both using US F5 (4.00 mm) hook. Change hook size, if necessary, to obtain these gauges.

abbreviations
4hdc puff stitch—[yrh, insert hook, yrh and pull loop through] 4 times, yrh and pull through 9 loops on hook. See also page 17.

note
■ When working the puff stitches pull the loops up until they are ¾ in. (2 cm) long.

band
Make 90ch, ss in first ch to form a ring.
1st round (WS): 1ch, [1sc in each ch] to end, ss in first sc, turn. 90 sts.
2nd round: 1ch, [1sc in each sc] to end, ss in first sc, turn.
2nd round forms sc.
Turning at the end of each round, work 3 more rounds sc.

top
Work in puff st patt.
1st round (RS): 1ch, 1hdc in same place as ss, 3ch, 4hdc puff st over hdc, 1ch, [skip 1sc, 1hdc in next sc, 3ch, 4hdc puff st over previous hdc, 1ch] 44 times, ss in first 3ch sp.
2nd round: 1ch, [2sc in each 3ch sp] to end, ss in first sc. 90 sts.
These 2 rounds form puff st patt.
Cont in puff st patt, work 9 more rounds.
12th round: 1ch, 2sc in first 3ch sp, 2sc in each of next two 3ch sps, [1sc in each of foll two 3ch sps, 2sc in each of next three 3ch sps]

to last two 3ch sps, 1sc in each of last two 3ch sps, ss in first sc. 72 sts.
13th round: As 1st round but working instructions in square brackets 35 times.
14th round: 1ch, 2sc in first 3ch sp, 2sc in next 3ch sp, [1sc in foll 3ch sp, 2sc in each of next two 3ch sps] to last 3ch sp, 1sc in last 3ch sp, ss in first sc. 60 sts.
15th round: As 1st round but working instructions in square brackets 29 times.
16th round: 1ch, 2sc in first 3ch sp, [1sc in each of next two 3ch sps,

tips

■ The hat is worked in rounds. The puff stitch pattern is worked with the RS facing for all rounds.

■ If you want to press your hat to open up the pattern, turn the hat inside out, stuff the hat with a rolled up towel and steam press lightly on the wrong side taking care not to squash the puffs.

grey

2sc in foll 3ch sp] to last two 3ch sps, 1sc in each of last two 3ch sps, ss in first sc.

40 sts.

17th round: As 1st round but working instructions in square brackets 19 times.

18th round: 1ch, 1sc in each 3ch sp, ss in first sc. 20 sts.

19th round: As 1st round but working instructions in square brackets 9 times.

20th round: 1ch, 1sc in each 3ch sp, ss in first sc. 10 sts.

21st round: As 1st round but working instructions in square brackets 4 times.

Fasten off.

Thread end through each 3ch sp, draw up and secure. Weave in ends.

lacy silk scarf

This sophisticated silk scarf is made from pretty, openwork motifs joined together and finished with a picot edging.

size
Actual measurements: width 5 in. (13 cm); length 57 in. (145 cm)

materials
3 x 1³/₄ oz. (50 g) hanks of Debbie Bliss Pure Silk in pale grey, shade 02
US E4 (3.50 mm) crochet hook

gauge
Each square measures 4³/₄ x 4³/₄ in. (12 x 12 cm) when pressed, using US E4 (3.50 mm) hook. Change hook size, if necessary, to obtain this size square.

abbreviations
See page 17.

note
■ The square motifs stretch into oblongs when worn.

lacy square
Make 6ch, ss in first ch to form a ring.

1st round (RS): 1ch, 16sc in ring, ss in first sc.

2nd round: 6ch, [skip 1sc, 1dc in next sc, 4ch] 7 times, skip last sc, ss in 3rd ch.

3rd round: 1ch, [1sc, 1hdc, 3dc, 1hdc, 1sc] in each sp.

4th round: 7ch, [1sc between last sc of nearest petal and first sc of next petal, 6ch] 7 times, ss in first ch.

5th round: 1ch, [1sc, 1hdc, 6dc, 1hdc, 1sc] in each 6ch sp.

6th round: Ss in back strand of next hdc and foll 2dc, [6ch, skip 2dc, 1sc in back strand of next dc, 6ch, 1sc in back strand of 2nd dc of next petal] 7 times, 6ch, skip 2dc, 1sc in back strand of next dc, 3ch, 1dc in 3rd ss.

7th round: 3ch, 3dc in dc sp, * 4ch, 1sc in next 6ch sp, [6ch, 1sc in foll 6ch sp] twice, 4ch, [4dc, 4ch, 4dc] in next 6ch sp, ** rep from * two more times, 4ch, 1sc in next 6ch sp, [6ch, 1sc in foll 6ch sp] twice,

4ch, 4dc in last sp, 4ch, ss in 3rd ch. Fasten off.

scarf
Make 1st lacy square as given.

Join motifs
Make 2nd lacy square as given to **, rep from * once, 4ch, 1sc in next 6ch sp, [6ch, 1sc in foll 6ch sp] twice, 4ch, 4dc in next 6ch sp, 2ch, with RS of both squares facing, 1sc in corresponding corner sp of 1st square, 2ch, 4dc in same sp of 2nd square, 2ch, 1sc in next ch sp of 1st square, 2ch, [1sc in next ch sp of 2nd square, 3ch, 1sc in next ch sp of 1st square, 3ch] twice, 1sc in next ch sp of 2nd square, 2ch, 1sc in next ch sp of 1st square, 2ch, 4dc in first ch sp of 2nd square, 2ch, 1sc in corner ch sp of 1st square, 2ch, ss in 3rd ch at start of 2nd square. Fasten off.
Make and join 10 squares in this way.

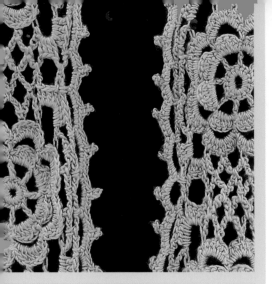

This
sophisticated
silk scarf is
made from
pretty,
openwork
flower motifs

tip

- There's no need to weave in the starting end; just lay it flat against the chain ring, work over it on the first round and snip it off.

edging

Join yarn in the right-hand corner sp of a motif near the center of one long edge.

1st round: 1ch, 1sc in same sp as join, 6ch, * 1sc in next sp, 6ch, rep from * to last corner sp of this edge, 3sc in corner sp, 6ch, rep from * 3 more times, then rep from * to end of round, ss in first sc.

2nd round: Ss in first 6ch sp, 1ch, * [3sc, 4ch, 1sc in 4th ch from hook, 3sc] in each 6ch sp along edge, at corner, work 1sc in each of first 2sc,

4ch, 1sc in 4th ch from hook, 1sc in last sc, rep from * 3 more times, then rep from * to end of round, ss in first sc.

Fasten off. Weave in ends. Press.

○	ch
+	sc
┬	hdc
┼	dc
•	ss

frills and flowers wrap

This flirty, frilly wrap is pure romance and so versatile. Because it increases out from a chain edge, it falls naturally into a spiral. You can pin it low on the shoulders like a little, lightweight cape, drape it over your arms like a stole, or swirl it around your neck like a scarf.

wrap

Make 122ch.

1st row (WS): 1sc in 2nd ch from hook, [1sc in each ch] to end. 121 sts.

2nd and 3rd rows: 1ch, [1sc in each sc] to end.

4th row (RS): 1sc in first sc, 1hdc in next sc, [2dc in next sc, 1dc in foll sc] 58 times, 2dc in next sc, 1hdc in foll sc, 1sc in last sc. 180 sts.

5th, 6th and 7th rows: 1sc in each of first 2 sts, 1hdc in each of next 3 sts, 1dc in each of foll 170dc, 1hdc in each of next 3 sts, 1sc in each of last 2 sts.

8th row: 1sc in each of first 2sc, 1hdc in each of next 3hdc, [4dcpc in next dc, 1dc in each of foll 2dc] 56 times, 4dcpc in next dc, 1hdc in each of next 3hdc, 1sc in next sc, 2sctog. 179 sts.

9th row: 1sc in each of first 2sc, 1hdc in each of next 3hdc, 1dc in each of foll 169 sts, 1hdc in each of next 3hdc, 1sc in each of last 2 sts.

10th row: 1sc in each of first 2sc, 1hdc in each of next 3hdc, [4dcpc in next dc, 2dc in each of foll 2dc]

56 times, 4dcpc in next dc, 1hdc in each of next 3hdc, 1sc in each of last 2sc. 291 sts.

11th row: 1sc in each of first 2sc, 1hdc in each of next 3hdc, 1dc in each of next 281 sts, 1hdc in each of next 3hdc, 1sc in each of last 2sc.

12th row: 1sc in each of first 2sc, 1hdc in each of next 3hdc, [4dcpc in next dc, 1dc in each of foll 4dc] 56 times, 4dcpc in next dc, 1hdc in each of next 3hdc, 1sc in each of last 2sc.

13th row: As 11th row.

14th row: 1ch, [1sc in each st] to end.

15th row: 1ch, 1sc in each of first 6sc, [3ch, skip 1sc, 1sc in next sc] 140 times, 1sc in each of last 5sc.

16th row: 1ch, 1sc in each of first 2sc, 1hdc in each of next 3sc, 1dc in foll sc, 3ch, 1dc in first 3ch sp, [3ch, 3dctog over previous dc, 1dc in next 3ch sp] 139 times, 3ch, 3dctog over previous dc, 3ch, 1dc in next sc, 1hdc in each of foll 3sc, 1sc in each of last 2sc.

17th row: 1ch, 1sc in first sc, [3ch,

size

Actual measurements: width 10¹/₂ in. (26.5 cm); length (at top edge) 39¹/₂ in. (100 cm)

materials

7 x ⁷/₈ oz. (25 g) balls of Sublime Kid Mohair Blend in Tundra, shade 0026
US 19 (5.50 mm) crochet hook

gauge

12 sts and 15 rows to 4 in. (10 cm) over single crochet, 11 sts and 6 rows to 4 in. (10 cm) over double and bobble pattern, both using US 19 (5.50 mm) hook. Change hook size, if necessary, to obtain these gauges.

abbreviations

3dctog—leaving last loop of each st on hook work 3dc, yrh and pull through 4 loops on hook.
4dcpc—work 4dc in place indicated, remove hook, insert in first dc, catch loop and pull through to close popcorn.
See also page 17.

skip one st, 1sc in foll st] twice, skip next st, [3ch, 1sc in next 3ch sp] 142 times, [3ch, skip one st, 1sc in foll st] 3 times. 147 sps.

18th row: Ss in first 3ch sp, 1ch, 5sc in first 3ch sp, [1sc in same place in row below as next sc, 5sc in next 3ch sp] 146 times. 881 sts.

19th row: [1sc, 2ch, 1dc] in first sc, 2dc in each of next 4sc, [skip next sc in row below, 2dc in each of foll 5sc] 146 times. 1470 sts.
Fasten off.

flowers (make 15)

Wind yarn around finger to form a ring.

1st round (RS): 1ch, 6sc in ring, remove hook, insert from front in first sc, catch loop and pull through to front.

2nd round: * [1ch, 1sc, 1hdc, 1dc, 1ch, 1dc, 1hdc, 1sc] in first sc, remove hook, insert from back in same sc, catch loop and pull through to back, remove hook, insert from front in next sc, catch loop and

pull through to front, repeat from * in each sc omitting last pull through to front.
Fasten off.

to finish

At each short end of wrap, gather row-ends, draw up and secure, then sew on a flower. Scatter remaining flowers over wrap and stitch in place.

tips

- The wrap is worked from the top down, so you don't need to work the starting chain loosely—just don't pull the chain so tight that it's hard to insert the hook on the first row.

- Ideally, you should always join in a new ball of yarn at the start of a row, but when the rows are as long as some of the ones in this wrap, it can be wasteful. Here are three ways of dealing with the ends. Firstly, if you have to leave a long end when joining in a new ball of yarn at the beginning of a row, use the long end to make a flower. Secondly, if you need to join in a new ball of yarn during a pattern row, hide the ends in one of the popcorns or bobbles. Thirdly, if you have to join in during a row, sew a flower on to hide the ends.

- Don't weave in the ends when making the flowers; instead, use them to sew on the flowers.

This flirty, frilly wrap is pure romance

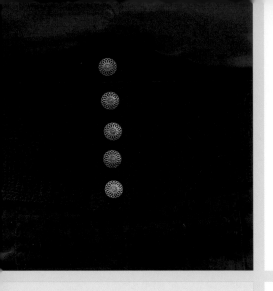

corset belt

This curvy corset belt has a panel of elastic at the back to make it flexible and to cut down on the amount of work you need to do. The buttons are decorative; the front fastens with hooks and eyes.

size

Actual measurements: waist 26(28:30:32) in. [66(71:76:81) cm]; width 5 in. (12.5 cm)
Figures in round brackets refer to larger sizes; one figure refers to all sizes.

materials

approximately 1¹/₂ (1⁷/₈:2:3¹/₈) oz. [45(50:55:60) g] of 4ply cotton in black
US 7 steel (1.50 mm) crochet hook
15³/₄ in. (40 cm) of 5 in. (12.5 cm)-wide black elastic
23¹/₂ in. (60 cm) black boning tape
8 in. (20 cm) hook and eye tape
sharp sewing needle
black sewing thread
5 buttons

gauge

32 sts and 34 rows to 4 in. (10 cm) over single crochet, before pressing, 29 rows to 4 in. (10 cm) when pressed, using US 7 steel (1.50 mm) hook. Change hook size, if necessary, to obtain this gauge.

abbreviations

See page 17.

note

■ When choosing which size to make, remember that the belt covers the ribs as well as the waist, so make sure you have room to breathe!

first side panel

Work 40 surface ch in a straight line 1 in. (2.5 cm) in from one short edge of the elastic.

1st row (WS): 1ch, 1sc in each ch. 40 sts.

2nd row: 1ch, [1sc in each sc] to end.

2nd row forms sc.

Work 43(51:59:65) more rows sc. Side panel measures 6(7:8:9) in. [15.5(18:20.5:23) cm] when pressed. Fasten off.

second side panel

Leaving 13³/₄ in. (35 cm) from first line of surface chain on the wide elastic, work 40 surface chain. Complete as first side.

to finish

Work a row of sc in the row-ends along the edges of each side panel. Press side panels, easing front edges to measure approximately 5¹/₂ in. (14 cm). Trim raw edges of elastic to ¹/₂ in. (1.5 cm). Cut two 5 in. (12.5 cm) pieces of boning tape and slip stitch over ends of elastic.

Placing a hook and eye as near as possible to each end, trim hook and eye tape to fit front edges, 6 hooks and eyes fitted the front edges of the belt in the picture. Cut two lengths of boning tape to fit front edges. Sew hook tape on one front edge and eye tape on the other front edge. Slip stitch the boning tapes over edges of hook and eye tapes. Sew on buttons between eyes, easing them over the front edge when fastening the hooks.

tips

■ The edges of the two side panels of crochet are contained at the join with the elastic but stretch naturally to approximately 5¹/₂ in. (14 cm) at the front edges, giving a curved effect without shaping.

■ If you can't get ready-made hook and eye tape, sew hooks and eyes at regular intervals on to ordinary seam tape.

grey

superlong scarf

A scarf this long has to be a real style statement. The stitch is very simple—just half double on every row—but the soft and tender yarn gives the pattern a lovely, lofty texture. Because the yarn is so thick, the scarf works up quickly despite the length. The ends are finished with pompoms as big as powder puffs.

size
Actual measurements: width 8 in. (20 cm); length (without pompoms) 95 in. (238 cm)

materials
7 x 1¾ oz. (50 g) balls of Sirdar Hug in Drift, shade 175
US 12 (8.00 mm) crochet hook

gauge
10 sts and 7 rows to 4 in. (10 cm) over half double using US 12 (8.00 mm) hook. Change hook size, if necessary, to obtain this gauge.

abbreviations
See page 17.

Make 21ch.

1st row: 1sc in 2nd ch from hook, [1sc in each ch] to end. 20 sts.
2nd row: 2ch, [1hdc in each sc] to end.
3rd row: 2ch, [1hdc in each hdc] to end.
3rd row forms hdc patt.
Cont in hdc for 164 more rows.
Last row: 1ch, [1sc in each hdc] to end.
Fasten off. Weave in ends.
Using a pompom maker or template 3½ in. (9 cm) in diameter with a 1½ in. (4 cm) center hole, make 2 pompoms.
Gathering each end of the scarf, sew on pompoms.

notes

- Work the starting chain very loosely.

- When working this hdc pattern the 2 turning chains are not counted as a stitch as this gives a neater edge.

tips

- When forming the stitches, do not pull the yarn taut; instead, work in a soft, loose way, turning the hook slightly as you pull through.

- If you prefer, you can measure your scarf instead of counting rows. If your tape measure isn't long enough, fold the scarf in half and measure 47 in. (119 cm).

- The best way to hide the ends when changing to a new ball of yarn is to work until 4 or 5 stitches from the edge, then using the old yarn, work the next half double until there are 3 loops on the hook and change to the new yarn to complete the stitch. Afterwards, weave the ends in, one to the left, the other to the right, along the row.

- Half double is very easy to do: take the yarn around the hook, insert in stitch, pull loop through, yarn around hook, pull through 3 loops on hook—that's all.

- Leave long ends when making the pompoms and use them to gather the scarf-ends and secure the pompoms.

grey

variation

For a completely different look from these instructions, you can make the scarf in worsted-weight wool yarn. I chose Colinette Cadenza in Bright Charcoal, shade 87 [you will need 3 x 1³/₄ oz. (50 g) hanks] for a striking random mix effect. Using a US F5 (4.00 mm) hook, my gauge was 20 stitches and 10 rows to 4 in. (10 cm) so the scarf measured 4 in. (10 cm) wide and 66 in. (167 cm) long before adding 3 small pompoms on each end.

grey

silver evening bag

This may look like a knitted fabric, but actually, it's all done with a crochet hook. Working surface chain on tapestry canvas is the easy-to-do trick that gives this pretty little bag a structured shape and a professional finish. Add lashings of crochet flowers, beads, and sequins to get you in the party mood.

size
Actual measurements: width 8 in. (20.5 cm); height 4¼ in. (11 cm)

materials
1 x 1¾ oz. (50 g) ball of 3ply (5 count) viscose and metallic yarn in silver
US 7 steel and US B1 (1.50 mm and 2.00 mm) crochet hooks
10¼ x 15 in. (26 x 38 cm) tapestry canvas [10 holes to 1 in. (2.5 cm)]
10¼ x 15 in. (26 x 38 cm) lining fabric
assorted silvery beads and sequins
one button
silver grey sewing thread
sharp sewing needle
39½ in. (1 m) silver braid
39½ in. (1 m) silver ribbon

gauge
40 sts to 4 in. (10 cm) over surface chain on 10 holes to 1 in. (2.5 cm) tapestry canvas using US 7 steel (1.50 mm) hook. Change hook size, if necessary, to fit through holes in canvas.

abbreviations
See page 17.

note
■ The US 7 steel (1.50 mm) hook used to work the surface chain had a fairly sharp point. Depending on the shape of the hook you use, you may need to use a smaller hook to pass through the holes easily.

front, back, and flap
Mark an area 82 holes wide and 128 holes long in the center of the canvas. Mark at each side of center 44 holes on lower edge, then mark 16 holes up from lower edge at each side. Join marks with a curved line to round off the corners of the front flap. Starting at 10th hole up from lower edge, mark an area 48 holes wide and 20 rows high in the center of the flap. This is left unworked for flower panel.
Using US 7 steel (1.50 mm) hook, work surface chain up and down in rows over the holes in the canvas, starting at top left corner (the top edge will be the front) and turning as necessary at the curved edges and the area marked on the flap.

side panels
Using US B1 (2.00 mm) hook, make 6ch.
1st row (WS): 1sc in 2nd ch from hook, [1sc in each ch] to end. 5 sts.
2nd row: 1ch, [1sc in each sc] to end.

2nd row forms sc. Work 1 more row sc.
Inc row: 1ch, 2sc in first sc, [1sc in each sc] to last sc, 2sc in last sc. 7 sts.
Cont in sc, inc in this way at each end of foll 4th row and next 2 RS rows. 13 sts.
Work 13 rows sc.
Dec row: 1ch, 2sctog, [1sc in each sc] to last 2sc, 2sctog. 11 sts.
Dec in this way at each end of next row. 9 sts.
Fasten off.

tip
■ The edges of the tapestry canvas can be quite sharp, so cover them with narrow masking tape to protect your hands and prevent the yarn snagging on the canvas.

flowers (make 9)

Using US B1 (2.00 mm) hook, wind yarn around finger to make a ring.

1st round: 1ch, 10sc in ring, remove hook, insert from front in first sc, catch loop and pull through to front.

2nd round: * [1ch, 1sc, 1hdc, 1dc, 1ch, 1dc, 1hdc, 1sc] in first sc, remove hook, insert from back in same sc, catch loop and pull through to back, remove hook, skip 1sc, insert hook from front in next sc, catch loop and pull through to front, rep from * 4 more times omitting last pull through to front.
Fasten off.

to finish

Trim canvas to within 3 or 4 holes from surface crochet. Turn edges in and press to hold in place. Allowing 1/2 in. (1.5 cm) all around for hem, place worked tapestry canvas on lining and mark hem edges. Press hems of lining to WS.

Sew the 9 flowers on the front panel and fill in all spaces between the flowers with beads and sequins. Leaving approximately 3 1/2 in. (9 cm) free for flap, set in side panels. Turn bag inside out. Sew ends of ribbon handle to underside at top of flap. Pin lining to front, back, and flap, stretching to fit and slip stitch in place around edges, removing pins as you work. Turn bag RS out. Pin braid around edge and stab stitch in place, removing pins as you work. Make a button loop at center of flap edge and sew button on front.

Add lashings of crochet flowers, beads, and sequins to get you in the party mood

tips

- Working surface chain on canvas is easy: simply hold the yarn under the canvas, insert the hook from the top in the first hole, catch the yarn and pull a loop through. Insert hook in next hole, catch yarn, pull through canvas and loop on hook. Each time you pull a chain through, tension the previous loop neatly against the canvas.

- The tapestry canvas may get a little bit crumpled as you work. Just press it lightly on the wrong side to restore the stiffness.

- To sew on sequins without the thread showing, bring the needle up in the center of the sequin, slip a tiny bead on to the needle and down to the sequin, then avoiding the bead, take the needle back through the hole in the sequin. Tension the thread and the bead will hold the sequin in place.

natural

Wild and woody earthy tones and neutral shades are the ultimate classic choices. Creamy oatmeal, caramel, bark brown, or bitter chocolate—wear them alone, contrast with cream, or spice them up with the colors of autumn in burnt orange, flame red, olive green, and golden yellow.

earflap hat

This classic earflap hat was inspired by a hat that friends brought back from Peru. It's worked in bands of striped single crochet and a simple two-color fan pattern.

size
Actual measurement around head 22 in. (56 cm)

materials
2 x 1¾ oz. (50 g) balls of Debbie Bliss Alpaca Silk DK in brown, shade 013 (A)
1 x 1¾ oz. (50 g) ball same in natural, shade 014 (B)
1 x 1¾ oz. (50 g) ball same in cream, shade 013 (C)
US F5 (4.00 mm) crochet hook

gauge
17 sts and 20 rows to 4 in. (10 cm) over single crochet stripe and double two-color patt using US F5 (4.00 mm) hook. Change hook size, if necessary, to obtain this gauge.

abbreviations
3dctog—leaving last loop of each st on hook, work 3dc, yrh and pull through 4 loops on hook.
See also page 17.

hat
Using A, wind yarn around finger to form a ring.
1st round (RS): 1ch, 6sc in ring, ss in first sc. 6 sts.
2nd round: 1ch, [1sc in each sc] to end, ss in first sc.
2nd round forms sc.
Work 2 more rounds sc.
5th round: 1ch, [2sc in each sc] to end, ss in first sc. 12 sts.
Cont in sc, work 1 more round in A, 1 round in B and 1 round in A.
9th round: 1ch, [2sc in each sc] to end, ss in first sc. 24 sts.
Cont in sc, work 1 round A, 1 round B and 3 rounds A.
15th round: Using B, 1ch, [1sc, 2ch, 1dc] in same place as ss, [using A, 3dctog, using B, 3dc in next sc] 5 times, using A, 3dctog, using B, 1dc in same place as first 2 sts, ss in 2nd ch.
Cont in A, work 1 round sc.
17th round: 1ch, 1sc in same place as ss, [2sc in next sc, 1sc in foll sc] 11 times, 2sc in last sc, ss in first sc.
36 sts.

Cont in sc, work 1 round A, 1 round C and 1 round A.
21st round: Using A, 1ch, 1sc in same place as ss, 1sc in next sc, [2sc in foll sc, 1sc in each of next 2sc] 11 times, 2sc in last sc, ss in first sc. 48 sts.
Cont in A, work 1 round sc.
23rd round: Using C, 1ch, [1sc, 2ch, 1dc] in same place as ss, [using A, 3dctog, using C, 3dc in next sc] 11 times, using A, 3dctog, using C, 1dc in same place as first 2 sts, ss in 2nd ch.
Cont in A, work 1 round sc.
25th round: 1ch, 1sc in same place as ss, 1sc in each of next 2sc, [2sc in foll sc, 1sc in each of next 3sc] 11 times, 2sc in last sc, ss in first sc. 60 sts.

notes
- The hat is worked in the round from the top down.
- When changing colors at the end of single crochet rounds, pull through the ss with the next color.

natural

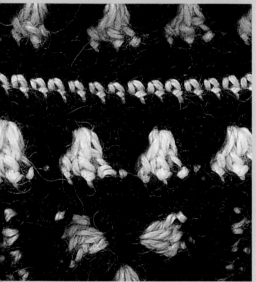

This cozy hat is worked in a simple two-color pattern

Cont in sc, work 1 round A, 1 round B and 1 round A.

29th round: Using A, 1ch, 1sc in same place as ss, 1sc in each of next 3sc, [2sc in foll sc, 1sc in each of next 4sc] 11 times, 2sc in last sc, ss in first sc. 72 sts.

Cont in A, work 1 round sc.

31st round: As 15th round, using B and A and working instructions in square brackets 17 times.

Cont in A, work 1 round sc.

33rd round: 1ch, 1sc in same place as ss, 1sc in each of next 4sc, [2sc in foll sc, 1sc in each of next 5sc] 11 times, 2sc in last sc, ss in first sc. 84 sts.

Cont in sc, work 1 round A, 1 round C, 1 round A.

37th round: Cont in A, 1ch, 1sc in same place as ss, 1sc in each of next 5sc, [2sc in foll sc, 1sc in each of next 6sc] 11 times, 2sc in last sc, ss in first sc. 96 sts.

Work 1 round sc.

39th round: As 15th round, using C and A and working instructions in square brackets 23 times.

Cont in sc, work 3 rounds A, 1 round B and 3 rounds A.

47th round: As 15th round, using B and A and working instructions in square brackets 23 times.

Cont in sc, work 3 rounds A, 1 round C and 3 rounds A.

55th round: As 15th round, using C and A and working instructions in square brackets 23 times.

notes

- When alternating colors in the same round, work the last pull through of the stitch before the color change in the next color. Allow the A yarn to lie on top of the sc that the 3dctog in B or C is worked into; it will fall quite naturally into place. Don't work over the B or C yarn: leave it at the top of the last dc ready to change color to complete the 3dctog in A.

- If you want to make the hat in two colors, you'll need 2 x 1¾ oz. (50 g) balls of A but only 1 x 1¾ oz. (50 g) ball of contrast for B and C.

- When making the tassel, leave long ends. Use the ends to sew the tassel on securely, then take the ends back down through the tassel and trim.

Cont in sc, work 2 rounds A.
Fasten off.

earflaps (make 2)

Using A, wind yarn around finger to form a ring.

1st round: 1ch, 6sc in ring, ss in first sc.

Cont in rows, working over color not in use on next row.

2nd row: Using A, 1ch, [1sc, 2ch] in same place as ss, using B, 3dc in same place as ss, [using A, 3dc in next sc, Using B, 3dc in foll sc] twice, using A, 1dc in same place as last 3dc in B, turn. 17 sts.

Cont in A.

3rd row: 1ch, 1sc in each of first 8dc,

3sc in next dc, 1sc in each of last 7dc, 1sc in 2nd ch. 19 sts.

4th row: 1ch, 1sc in each of first 9sc, 3sc in next sc, 1sc in each of last 9sc. 21 sts.

5th row: 1ch, 1sc in each of first 10sc, 3sc in next sc, 1sc in each of last 10sc. 23 sts.

6th row: Using B, 1ch, 1sc in each of first 11sc, 3sc in next sc, 1sc in each of last 11sc. 25 sts.

7th row: Using A, 1ch, 1sc in each of first 12sc, 3sc in next sc, 1sc in each of last 12sc. 27 sts.

Edging round (WS): Cont in A, 1ch, 1sc in each of first 13sc, 3sc in next sc, 1sc in each of next 12sc, 3sc in next sc, 1sc in each of next 4 row-ends, 2sc over next st of 2nd row, 2sc in next sc, 2sc over last st of 2nd row, 1sc in each of next 4 row-ends, 2sc in same place as first sc, ss in first sc.
Leaving a long end, fasten off.

edging

Mark sc at center back join, then mark 10sc at each side of center back sc. With RS facing, matching sts, use long ends to sew earflaps to next 18 sc at each side of markers. With RS facing and hat upside down, join A in center back sc.

1st round: 1ch, 1sc in same place as join, 1sc in each of next 10sc along back edge, * 1sc in each of first 14sc of earflap, 3sc in next sc, 1sc in each of last 14sc of earflap *, 1sc in each of next 39sc along front edge, rep from * to *, 1sc in each of last 10sc along back edge, ss in first sc. 122 sts.

2nd round: Using B, 1ch, 1sc in each of first 26sc, 3sc in next sc, 1sc in each of foll 69sc, 3sc in next sc, 1sc in each of last 25 sc, ss in first sc. 126 sts.
Fasten off.

to finish

Weave in ends. Using lengths of A and B, each approximately 55 in. (140 cm) long make a two color twisted cord. Knot and cut cord to give two 9 in. (22 cm) lengths. Sew cords on earflaps. Using A, make a fat tassel with a finished length of 4 in. (10 cm) and sew on point of hat.

plaid scarf

Here's a scrap yarn project that doesn't look like one! All you do is crochet a simple mesh grid in one color, then weave through as many contrast colors as you like to make a rich, soft fabric.

size
Actual measurements: width 10 in. (25 cm); length 57½ in. (146 cm)

materials
approximately 7 oz. (200 g) DK wool in camel (A)
approximately 1 oz. (25 g) fine mohair in each of black (B) and cream (C)
approximately 1 oz. (25 g) DK-weight mohair in each of orange (D) and ochre (E)
US F5 (4.00 mm) crochet hook
tapestry needle

gauge
10 x 1dc, 1ch sp and 8½ rows to 4 in. (10 cm) over checked mesh patt using US F5 (4.00 mm) hook. Change hook size, if necessary, to obtain this gauge.

abbreviations
See page 17.

note
■ The yarn amounts are approximate as the length of the yarns varies with the thickness. You should use a DK for the crochet, but for the weaving yarns, you can combine as many strands as you need to fill the holes in the grid.

scarf
Using A, make 52 ch.

1st row (WS): Working into strand at back of ch each time, 1sc in 2nd ch from hook, [1sc in each ch] to end. 51 sts.

2nd row: 1sc in first sc, 2ch, 1dc in each of next 2sc, * [1ch, skip 1sc, 1dc in next sc] twice, 1ch, skip 1sc **, 1dc in each of next 5sc, rep from * 3 more times, then rep from * to **, 1dc in each of last 3sc.

3rd row: 1sc in first sc, 2ch, 1dc in each of next 2dc, * [1ch, skip 1ch, 1dc in next dc] twice, 1ch, skip 1ch **, 1dc in each of next 5dc, rep from * 3 more times, then rep from * to **, 1dc in each of last 2dc, 1dc in 2nd ch.

4th row: As 3rd row.

5th row: 1sc in first dc, 2ch, 1ch, skip 1dc, 1dc in foll dc, * [1ch, skip 1ch, 1dc in next dc] twice, 1ch, skip 1ch **, [1dc in next dc, 1ch, skip 1dc] twice, 1dc in foll dc, rep from * 3 more times, then rep from * to **, 1dc in next dc, 1ch, skip 1dc, 1dc in 2nd ch.

6th row: 1sc in first dc, 3ch, [1dc in next dc, 1ch, skip 1ch] to last st, 1dc in 2nd ch.

7th row: As 6th row.

8th row: 1sc in first dc, 2ch, 1dc in next ch, 1dc in next dc, * [1ch, skip 1ch, 1dc in next dc] 3 times **, [1dc in next ch, 1dc in next dc] twice, rep from * 3 more times, then rep from * to **, 1dc in each of last 2ch.

tips

■ Work the foundation chain loosely and use a larger hook if necessary. Work the last row of single crochet fairly tightly and if necessary, use a smaller hook, so the width matches the first row.

■ You can combine any yarns and colors, but it's a good idea to use brushed mohair yarns for weaving so the strands cling together instead of slipping out of the mesh.

■ Plan your color scheme for the pattern by laying out and overlapping short lengths of yarn. When you find a combination that you like, stick it down with clear tape and keep it as a reference.

natural

A scrap yarn project that doesn't look like one!

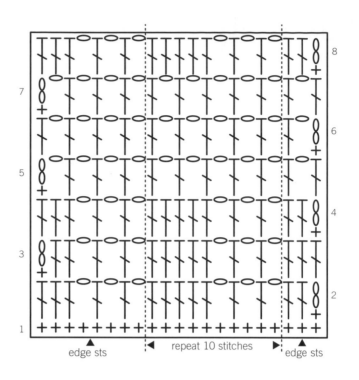

o	ch
+	sc
⊺	dc

edge sts · repeat 10 stitches · edge sts

3rd to 8th rows form the checked mesh patt.
Work 116 more rows in patt.
Work 1 row sc.
  Fasten off.

weaving

Weave along the length of the scarf first.

Stranding as many lengths together as necessary to comfortably fill the holes in the grid, cut 79 in. (2 m)-lengths of yarn as needed. Thread a tapestry needle with a group of strands and weave in and out up a line of holes. Continue until all vertical lines of holes have been filled, alternating colors to give a plaid effect as shown.

To weave across, cut 24 in. (61 cm)-lengths of yarn, using half the number of strands needed for the verticals. Hide the ends by starting weaving near the center of a horizontal line of holes; weave in and out to the side edge, taking the yarn around the edge; weave back across to the other side, taking the yarn around the edge; and weave until the ends overlap. Trim off any excess. To create the plaid effect, change colors in the same order as the vertical stripes.

When the checks are complete, knot the ends of the vertical strands and trim to make tassels.

natural

multiway wrap

This dramatic wrap is made from two long lengths of shell pattern crochet joined with a collar at the center. It's so versatile, you can wear it in lots of ways. Put your head through the collar and drape the ends over your shoulders for a cape effect, wind the ends around for a giant scarf, or wrap them around your body and pin to create a coat.

first side

Make 80ch.

1st row (WS): 1sc in 2nd ch from hook, [skip 2ch, 5dc in next ch, skip 2ch, 1sc in foll ch] to end. Thirteen 5dc shells.

2nd row: 3ch, 2dc in first sc, [skip 2dc, 1sc in next dc, skip 2dc, 5dc in next sc] to end, omitting last 2dc of last shell.

3rd row: 1ch, 1sc in first dc, [skip 2dc, 5dc in next sc, skip 2dc, 1sc in next dc] to end, working last sc in 3rd ch.

2nd and 3rd rows form the shell patt.

Cont in shell patt, work 67 more rows.

shell edging

Left side: 5dc in same sc as last 3dc of last row, [1sc in sc at base of next half shell, 5dc in sc at base of foll half shell] to end, 1sc in sc of first row. Fasten off.

Right side: Join yarn to the other end of first sc row. Starting 1ch, 1sc in same place as join, work to match left side, ending 5dc in

size
Actual measurements: width 10 in. (25 cm); length 57½ in. (146 cm)

materials
14 x 1¾ oz. (50 g) balls of Debbie Bliss Donegal Luxury Aran Tweed in natural, shade 07
US K10½ (7.00 mm) crochet hook
large button
large safety pin

gauge
12 sts (two shell patterns) to 3½ in. (9 cm), 7 rows to 4 in. (10 cm) over shell patt using US K10½ (7.00 mm) hook. Change hook size, if necessary, to obtain this gauge.

abbreviations
See page 17.

note
■ The wrap is made in two halves so the shell pattern runs out from the center join.

same sc as last half shell, ss in top
of 3ch. Fasten off.

second side

Work as given for first side.

tips

- It's easier to count the rows if you
  mark the RS of the work when you
  turn at the end of the 1st row.

- In a stitch pattern like this, the
  best place to join in a new ball of
  yarn is while working the last pull
  though of one of the 5 doubles
  that make a shell. When you
  weave in the ends, hide them in
  the shell pattern.

to finish

Placing chain edges together and
leaving 5 shells of each side free
at center, join ends of edgings and
4 shells of each side together with
sc on WS.

collar

Join yarn at neck edge in ch at base
of 5dc shell after seam.

1st round: Along 1st side of neck work
[3ch, 2dc] in same place as join,
[1sc in sc at base of next 5dc shell
of 2nd row, 5dc in ch at base of next
5dc shell of 1st row] 4 times, 1sc in
sc at base of last free 5dc shell of
2nd row, 5dc in seam sc, along 2nd
side of neck work 1sc in sc at base

*This dramatic
wrap is made
from two long
lengths of shell
pattern crochet
joined with a
collar at the
center. It's so
versatile, you
can wear it in
lots of ways*

natural

You'll probably invent a few more ways to wear this wrap— you won't be able to do without it!

of first 5dc shell of 2nd row, [5dc in ch at base of next 5dc shell of 1st row, 1sc in sc at base of next 5dc shell of 2nd row] 5 times, 5dc in seam sc, 1sc in sc at base of first side 5dc shell, 2dc in same place as join, ss in 3rd ch, turn. 12 shells.

2nd round: 1ch, 1sc in same place as join, [5dc in next sc, skip 2dc, 1sc in next dc, skip 2dc] 11 times, 5dc in last sc, ss in first sc, turn.

3rd round: [3ch, 2dc] in same place as join, [skip 2dc, 1sc in next dc, skip 2dc, 5dc in next sc] 11 times, skip 2dc, 1sc in next dc, skip 2dc,

2dc in same place as first 3 sts, ss in 3rd ch, turn.

2nd and 3rd rounds form shell patt in the round to match shell patt in rows. Work 4 more rounds. Fasten off. Weave in ends.

Button backing

Wind yarn around finger to form a ring. 1ch, 8sc in ring, ss in first sc. Fasten off. Use ends to sew button onto backing. Place button on RS and pin through backing.

natural

slipper boots

These cozy slippers are shaped like boots with an extra layer in the soles to cushion your feet. The brown yarn is shaded so it looks like suede, and though the cuffs and trims are worked in a textured stitch to look like sheepskin, it's all just simple crochet.

size
Actual measurements: length of sole 9½(10½:11) in. [24(26:28) cm]; around boot top 11¾ in. (30 cm) Figures in round brackets refer to larger sizes; one figure refers to all sizes.

materials
4 x 1¾ oz. (50 g) balls of Sirdar Peru in Prairie, shade 309 (A)
2 x 1¾ oz. (50 g) balls of Sirdar Peru in Llama, shade 306 (B)
US F5 (4.00 mm) crochet hook
pair of insoles

gauge
14 sts and 15 rows to 4 in. (10 cm) over single crochet using US F5 (4.00 mm) hook. Change hook size, if necessary, to obtain this gauge.

abbreviations
3hdc puff st—[yrh, insert hook in st pull loop through and elongate loop to height of a dc] 3 times, yrh and pull though 7 loops on hook.
See also page 17.

left boot
outer sole
Using A, make 7ch.

1st row (RS): 1sc in 2nd ch from hook, [1sc in each ch] to end. 6 sts.
2nd row: 1ch, 2sc in first sc, 1sc in each of next 4sc, 2sc in last sc. 8 sts.
3rd row: 1ch, 2sc in first sc, 1sc in each of next 6sc, 2sc in last sc. 10 sts.
4th row: 1ch, [1sc in each sc] to end. 4th row forms sc. Cont in sc, work 12 more rows **.

shape instep
Inc row (RS): 1ch, [1sc in each sc] to last sc, 2sc in last sc. 11 sts.
Cont in sc, inc in this way at end of next 3(4:5) RS rows. 14(15:16) sts.
Work 8(9:10) rows sc.

shape toe
Dec row: 1ch, 2sctog, [1sc in each sc] to last 2sc, 2sctog. 12(13:14) sts.
Work 1 row sc.
Dec in same way as before at each end of next 3 rows. 6(7:8) sts.
Fasten off.

inner sole
Using B, work as outer sole.

boot top
Using B, make 42ch, ss in first ch to form a ring.

1st round: 1ch, [1sc in each ch] to end, ss in first sc, turn. 42 sts.
2nd round: 1sc in same place as ss, 2ch, [3hdc puff st in next sc, 1tr in foll sc] 20 times, 3hdc puff st in last sc, ss in 2nd ch, turn.
3rd round: 1ch, [1sc in each st] to end, turn.
4th and 5th rounds: As 2nd and 3rd rounds.

leg
Change to A. Noting that 1st round will be a WS round, turning each time, work 33 rounds sc same way as 3rd round, so ending with a WS round.
Fasten off ***.

heel
Fold leg in half with join in rounds at outside center left. With RS facing,

natural

These cozy slippers are shaped like boots with an extra layer in the soles

join yarn in 9th sc before join in last round.

1st row (RS): 1ch, 1sc in same place as join, 1sc in each of next 37sc, turn leaving 4sc of last round of leg. 38 sts.

Cont in sc, dec in same way as sole at each end of next 2 rows. 34 sts. Work 5 rows sc. Fasten off.

upper

With RS of leg facing, join A in last row-end on the right of the heel.

1st row (RS): 1ch, 1sc in same place as join, 1sc in each of next 7 row-ends, 1sc in same sc as last row-end, 1sc in each of next 4sc of leg, 1sc in same sc as first row-end of heel, 1sc in each of next 8 row-ends. 22 sts.

Work 16(19:22) rows sc.

shape toe

1st row: 1ch, 1sc in each of first 3sc, 2sctog, 1sc in each of next 12sc, 2sctog, 1sc in each of last 3sc. 20 sts.

2nd row: 1ch, 2sctog, [1sc in each sc] to last 2sc, 2sctog. 18 sts.

3rd row: 1ch, [2sctog] twice, [1sc in each sc] to last 4sc, [2sctog] twice. 14 sts.

4th row: As 2nd. 12 sts.

5th row: As 3rd. 8 sts.

6th row: As 2nd. 6 sts.

Fasten off.

right boot

Outer sole

Work as left boot outer sole to **.

shape instep

Inc row (RS): 1ch, 2sc in first sc, [1sc in each sc] to end. 11 sts. Cont in sc, inc in this way at beg of next 3(4:5) RS rows. 14(15:16) sts. Complete as left outer sole.

inner sole

Using B, work as outer sole.

boot top

Work as given for left boot.

heel

Fold leg in half with join in rounds at outside center right. With RS facing, join yarn in 14th sc after join in last round.

Complete as left heel.

natural

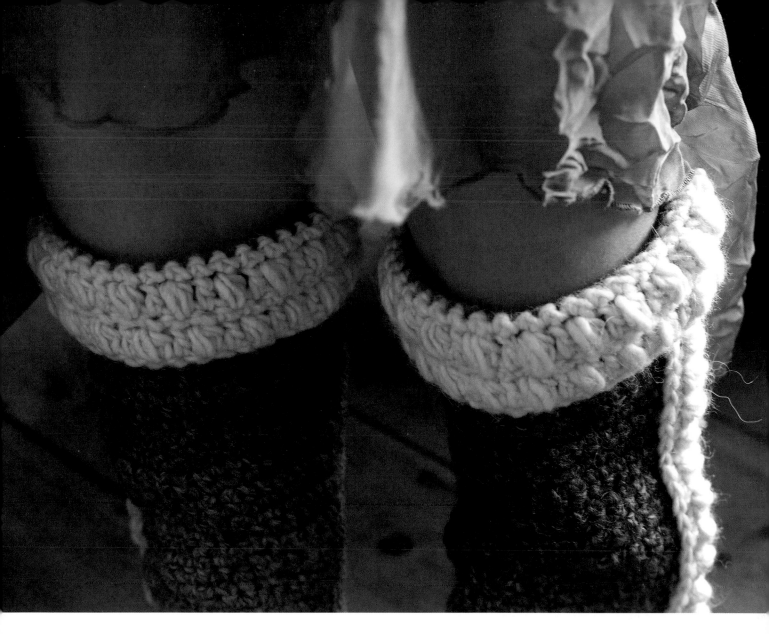

upper

Work as left boot upper.

to finish

Trim insoles to fit just inside outer sole. Using A and inserting insole between outer sole in A below and inner sole in B above, join soles with a round of sc. Using A, work surface chain as close to the edge as possible over the round of sc in A. With sole in B above and RS of top facing, pin upper part of boot to sole,

sew tops to soles, removing pins. Weave in ends.

trims (make 2)

Using B, make 34ch.

1st row: Working into strand at back of ch each time, 1sc in 2nd ch from hook, [1sc in each ch] to end. 33 sts.

2nd row: 1sc in first sc, 2ch, [3hdc puff st in next sc, 1dc in foll sc] to end.

3rd row: 1ch, 1sc in each st.

Fasten off. Sew trims to sides of boots to cover the join in rounds. Fold to RS.

flower fingerless gloves

These pretty mitts are designed to use up odd scraps of yarn. They're very simply constructed: you make the motifs, then work a band of single crochet around the hand with a hole for the thumb. Finish off the top with finger openings and the lower edge with a shell trim.

size
Actual measurements: around hand 7 in. (18 cm); length 5½ in. (14 cm)

materials
approximately 2 oz. (50 g) Shetland style wool 4ply in natural (E)
a total of approximately 1 oz. (25 g) same in red (A), yellow (B), orange (C) and green (D)
US D3 (3.00 mm) crochet hook
tapestry needle

gauge
Four flower motif measures 2¾ x 2¾ in. (7 x 7 cm), 24 sts and 27 rows to 4 in. (10 cm) over single crochet using US D3 (3.00 mm) hook. Change hook size, if necessary, to obtain this size motif and this gauge.

abbreviations
See page 17.

four flower motif (make 2)
1st flower
Using A, wind yarn around finger to form a ring.
Petal round (RS): [1ch, 1sc, 1dc, 1ch, 1dc, 1sc, ss in ring] 4 times.
Fasten off.

2nd flower
Using B, work as 1st flower.

3rd flower
Using C, work as 1st flower until first dc of 2nd petal has been completed, elongate loop on hook and remove hook, with WS tog, insert hook in a 1ch sp of a petal in flower in A, catch loop and pull through to join flowers, tighten loop on hook and cont until first dc of 4th petal has been completed, join to a 1ch sp of a petal in flower in B in same way as before, complete 4th petal.
Fasten off.

4th flower
As 3rd flower, joining 2nd and 4th petals to flowers in A and B to form a square with 4 free petals at the center.

With WS of flowers facing, join D in a 1ch sp of a center petal.

center round
1ch, 1sc in same place as join, [1sc in 1ch sp of next free petal] 3 times, ss in first sc. Fasten off.
With RS facing, join E in 1ch sp of corner petal in B.

edging
1st round: [1ch, 1sc, 2ch, 1sc] in same place as join, * 3ch, 1sc in 1ch sp of next petal of same flower, 1ch, 1sc in 1ch sp of adjacent petal of next flower, 3ch **, [1sc, 2ch, 1sc] in 1ch sp of corner petal of same flower, rep from * two more times, then rep from * to **, ss in first sc.
2nd round: Ss in first 2ch sp, [1ch, 1sc, 2ch, 1sc] in same 2ch sp, * 1sc in next sc, 3sc in 3ch sp, 1sc in next sc, 1sc in 1ch sp, 1sc in foll sc, 3sc in 3ch sp, 1sc in next sc **, [1sc, 2ch, 1sc] in corner 2ch sp, rep from * two more times, then rep from * to **, ss in first sc. Fasten off.
3rd round: Join D in corner 2ch sp, * 1ch, [1sc, 2ch, 1sc] in corner 2ch sp,

These pretty mitts are designed to use up odd scraps of yarn

1sc in each of next 13sc, rep from *
3 more times, ss in first sc.
Fasten off.

left glove

palm

With RS facing join E in corner 2ch
sp of motif next to flower in B.
1st row: 1ch, 1sc in same 2ch sp,
1sc in each of next 15sc, 1sc in next
2ch sp.
17 sts.
2nd row: 1ch, [1sc in each sc]
to end.
2nd row forms sc.
Work 2 more rows sc.

thumb opening

1st row (RS): 1ch, 1sc in each of next
5sc, 7ch, skip 7sc, 1sc in each of
next 5sc.
2nd row: 1ch, 1sc in each of first 5sc,
1sc in each of next 7ch, 1sc in each
of last 5sc. 17 sts.
Work 24 rows sc.
Leaving a long end, fasten off.
Thread tapestry needle with long end
and with RS facing, taking one st
from each side each time, starting
and ending in 2ch sp, join last row to
the other edge of the motif.

top

With flower in A at top left, join E in
last row-end of palm.
1st round (RS): 1ch, 1sc in same
place as join, 1sc in each of next
29 row-ends, 1sc in corner 2ch sp,
1sc in each of next 15sc, 1sc in next

corner 2ch sp, ss in first sc, turn.
47 sts.
2nd round: 1ch, [1sc in each sc] to
end, ss in first sc, turn.
2nd round forms sc. Turning each
time, work 1 more round E, 1 round
D and 2 rounds E ***. Cont in E.

4th finger

1ch, 1sc in each of first 8sc, skip
next 36 sc, 1sc in each of last 3sc,
ss in first sc, turn. 11 sts. Work
1 round sc. Fasten off.

3rd finger

Join E in first free sc of palm. 1ch, 1sc in each of first 6sc, skip 24sc, 1sc in each of last 6sc, ss in first sc, turn. 12 sts. Work 1 round sc. Fasten off.

2nd finger

As 3rd finger but skipping 12sc.

1st finger

As 3rd finger working on last 12sc.

thumb

Join E in first free sc at lower edge of thumb opening.

1st round: 1ch, 1sc in each of 7sc up first side, 2sc in row-end, 1sc in base of each of 7ch down 2nd side, 2sc in row-end, ss in first sc, turn. 18 sts.
Turning each time, work 3 more rounds sc. Fasten off.

finger and thumb edgings

Work 1 round sc in A.

lower edging

Work in same way as top to ***, so ending with a WS round. Cont in E.

Next round (RS): 1ch, 1sc in same place as join, 1sc in each of next 2sc, [2sctog, 1sc in each of next 2sc] 11 times, ss in first sc, turn. 36 sts.
Work 3 more rounds sc. Change to A.

shell edging

1ch, [skip 1sc, 5dc in next sc, skip 1sc, ss in next sc] 9 times, ending ss in first ch. Fasten off.
Weave in ends.

right glove

palm

Join D in corner 2ch sp of motif next to flower in C.
Complete as left glove.

top

With flower in A at top right, join D in first 2ch sp of motif.

1st round (RS): 1ch, 1sc in same place as join, 1sc in each of next 15sc, 1sc in corner 2ch sp, 1sc in each of next 30 row-ends, ss in first sc, turn. 47 sts.
Complete top as left glove.

4th finger

1ch, 1sc in each of first 3sc, skip 36sc, 1sc in each of last 8sc, ss in first sc, turn.
11 sts.
Complete 4th finger and work 3rd, 2nd and 1st fingers to match left glove.

thumb

Join E in base of first free ch at lower edge of thumb opening.

1st round: 1ch, 1sc in base of each of 7ch up first side, 2sc in row-end, 1sc in each 7sc down 2nd side, 2sc in row-end, ss in first sc, turn. 18 sts.
Complete thumb and work finger and thumb edgings and lower edging as given for left glove.

blue

For the ultimate in casual chic, there's nothing like blue. Whatever the shade—from deepest navy through to denim, bright blue, or turquoise—they'll all go with your jeans. For a fresh sporty look, contrast with black or add stripes of cream, sky, and magenta.

two-tone gloves

I based the idea for working these gloves with a separate back and front on traditional riding or driving gloves. Working the gloves into flat, or almost flat, pieces is very easy, but the result is very unusual. You can vary the length of the gloves or choose to make them without fingers.

size

Actual measurements: around hand 7¹/₂(8¹/₄) in. [19(21) cm]; length from cuff to start of fingers (long) 6 in. (15 cm); (short) 4¹/₈ in. (10.5 cm)
Figures in round brackets refer to larger size, one figure refers to both sizes.

materials

approximately 2¹/₂ oz. (70 g) of wool mix 4ply in black (A)
approximately 1³/₄ oz. (50 g) of wool mix 4ply in blue (B)
US D3 (3.00 mm) crochet hook

gauge

24 sts and 26 rows to 4 in. (10 cm) over single crochet using US D3 (3.00 mm) hook. Change hook size, if necessary, to obtain this gauge.

abbreviations

See page 17.

left glove front

Using A, make 19(23)ch.
1st row (WS): 1sc in 2nd ch from hook, [1sc in each ch] to end. 18(22) sts.
2nd row: 1ch, [1sc in each sc] to end.
2nd row forms sc **.
Work 3 more rows sc.
Dec row (RS): 1ch, 2sctog, [1sc in each sc] to last 2sc, 2sctog. 16(20) sts.
Cont in sc, dec in this way at each end of next RS row. 14(18) sts.
Work 3 rows sc.
Inc row (RS): 1ch, 2sc in first sc, [1sc in each sc] to last sc, 2sc in last sc. 16(20) sts.
Cont in sc, inc in this way at each end of next RS row. 18(22) sts.
*** Work 1 row sc.

shape thumb

1st row (RS): 1ch, [1sc in each of first 14(17)sc, 3sc in next sc, 1sc in each of last 3(4)sc. 20(24) sts.
2nd and every WS row: 1ch, [1sc in each sc] to end.
3rd row: 1ch, 1sc in each of first 14(17)sc, 2sc in next sc, 1sc in foll sc, 2sc in next sc, 1sc in each of last 3(4)sc. 22(26) sts.
5th row: 1ch, 1sc in each of first 14(17)sc, 2sc in next sc, 1sc in each of foll 3sc, 2sc in next sc, 1sc in each of last 3(4)sc. 24(28) sts.
7th row: 1ch, 1sc in each of first 14(17)sc, 2sc in next sc, 1sc in each of foll 5sc, 2sc in next sc, 1sc in each of last 3(4)sc. 26(30) sts.
9th row: 1ch, 1sc in each of first 14(17)sc, 2sc in next sc, 1sc in each

notes

- The wool mix 4ply used for the gloves is often called sock yarn. It's 75% wool, 25% polyamide and has 275 yards (250 meters) to a 3¹/₂ oz. (100 g) ball.

- Instructions are given for the long gloves shown in black and blue with the short gloves given as a variation, shown as fingerless mitts in two shades of grey.

- Adjust the length of the fingers by measuring them against your own fingers and working more or less rows straight as necessary.

blue

tips

- Working the line of surface chain around the edge of the back of the glove gives a much neater join than just working single crochet over both edges. Do take care not to pull the surface chain tight, or else it's hard to insert the hook. If necessary, use a smaller hook to work the single crochet join.

- To cut down on the amount of ends to weave in, if you're making fingerless gloves, leave very long ends when fastening off for the fingers, then use the ends when joining the back and front.

of foll 7sc, 2sc in next sc, 1sc in each of last 3(4)sc.
28(32) sts.
Work 6 rows sc.

thumb opening

1st row (RS): 1ch, 1sc in each of first 14(17)sc, 6ch, skip 11sc, 1sc in each of last 3(4)sc.

2nd row: 1ch, 1sc in each of first 3(4)sc, 1sc in each of next 6ch, 1sc in each of last 14(17)sc. 23(27) sts.

3rd row: 1ch, 1sc in each of first 14(17)sc, 2sctog, 1sc in each of foll 2sc, 2sctog, 1sc in each of last 3(4)sc. 21(25) sts.

4th row: 1ch, 1sc in each of first 2(3)sc, 2sctog, 1sc in foll sc, 2sctog, 1sc in each of last 14(17)sc. 19(23) sts.
Work 7 rows sc.

1st finger

1st row (WS): 1ch, 1sc in each of first 6(7)sc, 3ch, turn.

2nd row: 1sc in 2nd ch from hook, 1sc in next ch, 1sc in each of 6(7)sc. 8(9) sts.
Cont in sc, work 13 rows straight, then work 2sctog at each end of next 3 RS rows. 2(3) sts. Fasten off.

2nd finger

With WS facing, join A in base of 2nd ch at inner edge of 1st finger.

1st row (WS): 1ch, 1sc in base of same ch as join, 1sc in base of next ch, 1sc in each of next 5(6)sc of front, 3ch, turn.

2nd row: 1sc in 2nd ch from hook, 1sc in next ch, 1sc in each of next 7(8)sc. 9(10) sts.
Cont in sc, work 15 rows straight, then work 2sctog at each end of next 3 RS rows. 3(4) sts. Fasten off.

3rd finger

With WS facing, join A in base of 2nd ch at inner edge of 2nd finger.

1st row (WS): 1ch, 1sc in same ch as join, 1sc in base of next ch, 1sc in each of next 4(5)sc of front, 3ch, turn.

2nd row: 1sc in 2nd ch from hook, 1sc in next ch, 1sc in each of next 6(7)sc. 8(9) sts. Complete as 1st finger.

4th finger

With WS facing, join yarn in base of 2nd ch at inner edge of 3rd finger.

1st row (WS): 1ch, 1sc in same ch as join, 1sc in base of next ch, 1sc in each of last 4(5)sc of front. 6(7) sts.
Cont in sc, work 12 rows, then work 2sctog at each end of next 2 RS rows. 2(3) sts. Fasten off.

left glove back

Using B, make 20(21) ch.

1st row (WS): 1sc in 2nd ch from hook, [1sc in each ch] to end. 19(20) sts.
Noting that there is one less (two more) st(s), work as given for front to ***.
Work 26 rows sc, ending with a RS row.

4th finger

1st row (WS): 1ch, 1sc in each of first 4sc, turn. 4 sts.
Cont in sc, work 13 rows, then work

[2sctog] twice on next row. 2 sts.
Fasten off.

3rd finger

With WS facing, join yarn in next free sc of back.

1st row: 1ch, 1sc in same sc as join, 1sc in each of next 4sc, turn. 5 sts. Cont in sc work 17 rows, then work 2sctog at each end of next row. 3 sts.
Fasten off.

2nd finger

With WS facing, join yarn in next free sc of back.

1st row: 1ch, 1sc in same sc as join, 1sc in each of next 4(5)sc, turn. 5(6) sts.
Cont in sc work 19 rows, then work 2sctog at each end of next row. 3(4) sts.
2nd size only Work [2sctog] twice on next row.
Both sizes Fasten off.

1st finger

Work on last 5sc of back as given for 3rd finger.

right glove

Work front and back to match left glove reversing thumb shaping and fingers.

to finish

Press according to ball band.
Using A and with RS facing, starting and finishing at chain edge, work a line of surface chain around the back of each glove spaced evenly as close as possible to the edge.
Fasten off.
With WS together, pin backs and fronts of gloves together.
Using A and removing pins as you work, join each back and front together with a row of sc, taking hook under ss on back and over the edge of corresponding row or st on front, working twice into ss at fingertips as necessary.
Weave in ends.

variation
two tone mitts

To make the shorter, fingerless mitts shown here, you'll need around 1 oz. (30 g) of the same kind of yarn as the long gloves in dark grey (A) for the fronts and 7/8 oz. (25 g) in light grey (B) for the backs.

For short gloves, work as given for long gloves to **, then continue from *** to end. For fingerless gloves, divide for fingers and finish thumb as given but work only 3 rows sc before fastening off.

striped scarf

I decided to work this scarf sideways because I wanted to make it easy for you to be able to adapt it to your own varsity colors. All you need to do is change the width of the stripes and work them in the colors of your choice, see below for more details.

size
Actual measurements: width 7 in. (18 cm); length 68 in. (173 cm)

materials
4 x 1³/₄ oz. (50 g) balls of Debbie Bliss Cashmerino Aran in navy, shade 207 (A)
1 x 1³/₄ oz. (50 g) ball same in each of bright blue, shade 208 (B); pale blue, shade 207 (C); cream, shade 201 (D); and magenta, shade 616 (E)
US H8 (5.00 mm) crochet hook

gauge
15 sts and 22 rows to 4 in. (10 cm) over single crochet using US H8 (5.00 mm) hook. Change hook size, if necessary, to obtain this gauge.

abbreviations
See page 17.

scarf
Using A, make 261ch.
1st row: Working into strand at back of ch each time, 1sc in 2nd ch from hook, [1sc in each ch] to end. 260 sts.
2nd row: 1ch, [1sc in each sc] to end.
2nd row forms sc.
Cont in sc work 4 more rows A, * 2 rows B, 2 rows C, 2 rows D and 2 rows E *, work 12 rows A, rep from * to *, work 6 rows A.
Fasten off. Weave in ends.

notes

- It is essential to work the starting chain very loosely. Gently lengthen each chain as you make it, taking care that they are all the same size. Or, use a hook one or two sizes larger so the gauge of the chain matches the stitch gauge.

- Do not count the 1ch at the start of each row as a stitch.

tip

- 1 x 1³/₄ oz. (50 g) ball of Cashmerino Aran will work 6 rows of the scarf, so if you want a wider scarf, there will be enough yarn to work 3 rows of each of the contrast stripes, giving a scarf that will measure almost 8¹/₄ in. (21 cm).

how to adapt the stripes
Including the first row worked into the chain, there are 40 rows of single crochet in the scarf. So all you need to do is divide these 40 rows to give the number of stripes you need in each of your school varsity colors. To estimate the amount of yarn to buy, allow one ball of yarn for each 6 rows in a color. As a guide to when to change colors, simply mark off 40 squares on a sheet of graph paper, color in your choice of stripes, and mark off the rows as you work them.

beanie hat

This neat little hat is simple to make but has a few tricks that make it not just your average pull-on beanie. First of all, it starts at the top with a motif, a pretty way of getting through the first increase rounds quickly. Second, the main part is all in single crochet with rounds without increases worked in a spiral to give a professional finish. The flowers are optional.

size
Actual measurement around head 20½ in. (52.5 cm)

materials
2 x 1¾ oz. (50 g) balls of Sublime Soya Cotton DK in Indigo, shade 0080 (A)
1 x 1¾ oz. (50 g) ball same in Comfrey, shade 0084 (B)
US D3 and US E4 (3.00 mm and 3.50 mm) crochet hooks

gauge
Motif measures 3 in. (7.5 cm) across using US D3 (3.00 mm) hook, 17 sts and 20 rows to 4 in. (10 cm) over sc in rounds using US E4 (3.50 mm) hook. Change hook sizes, if necessary, to obtain this size motif and this gauge.

abbreviations
3dctog—leaving last loop of each st on hook, work 3dc, yrh and pull through 4 loops on hook.
4dctog—leaving last loop of each st on hook, work 4dc, yrh and pull though 5 loops on hook.
See also page 17.

note
■ The hat is worked from the top down.

motif
Using US D3 (3.00 mm) hook and A, make 5ch, ss in first ch to form a ring.
1st round (RS): 3ch, 19 dc in ring, ss in 3rd ch. 20 sts.
2nd round: 1ch, 1sc in same place as ss, [3ch, skip 1dc, 1sc in next dc] 9 times, 3ch, skip last dc, ss in first sc.
3rd round: Ss in first 3ch sp, 2ch, 3dctog in same 3ch sp, [4ch, 4dctog in next 3ch sp] 9 times, 4ch, ss in 3dctog.

crown
Change to US E4 (3.50mm) hook.
4th round: 1ch, 1sc in 3dctog, [4sc in next 4ch sp, 1sc in next 4dctog] 9 times, 4sc in last 4ch sp, ss in first sc.
50 sts.
5th round: 1ch, 2sc in same place as ss, [1sc in each of next 9sc, 2sc in foll sc] 4 times, 1sc in each of last 9sc, ss in first sc.
55 sts.
6th round: 1ch, 2sc in same place as ss, [1sc in each of next 10sc, 2sc in

foll sc] 4 times, 1sc in each of last 10sc, ss in first sc.
60 sts.
7th round: 1ch, 2sc in same place as ss, [1sc in each of next 11sc, 2sc in foll sc] 4 times, 1sc in each of last 11sc, ss in first sc.
65 sts.
8th round: 1ch, 2sc in same place as ss, [1sc in each of next 12sc, 2sc in foll sc] 4 times, 1sc in each of last 12sc, ss in first sc.
70 sts.
9th, 11th, 13th and 15th rounds: 1ch, [1sc in each sc] to end, ss in first sc.
10th round: 1ch, 2sc in same place as ss, [1sc in each of next 13sc, 2sc in foll sc] 4 times, 1sc in each of last 13sc, ss in first sc.
75 sts.
12th round: 1ch, 2sc in same place as ss, [1sc in each of next 14sc, 2sc in foll sc] 4 times, 1sc in each of last 14sc, ss in first sc.
80 sts.
14th round: 1ch, 2sc in same place as ss, [1sc in each of next 15sc, 2sc in foll sc] 4 times, 1sc in each of last

blue

This neat little hat is simple to make but has a few tricks that make it not just your average pull-on beanie

15sc, ss in first sc.
85 sts.

16th round: 1ch, 2sc in same place as ss, [1sc in each of next 16sc, 2sc in foll sc] 4 times, 1sc in each of last 16sc, ss in first sc.
90 sts.

Cont as given for 9th round but omitting ss at end to work in a spiral, work 18 rounds sc.

brim

Next round: 2sc in first sc, [1sc in each of next 8sc, 2sc in foll sc] 9 times, 1sc in each of last 8sc.
100 sts.

Work 9 rounds sc.

Next round: [2sctog, 1sc in each of next 8sc] 10 times. 90 sts.

Work 1 more round sc, ending ss in first sc.

Fasten off.

flowers (make 3)

Using US E4 (3.50mm) hook and B wind yarn around finger to form a ring.

1st round (RS): 1ch, 5sc in ring, pull end to close ring, remove hook, insert in front of first sc, catch loop and pull through.

2nd round: * [1ch, 1sc, 1hdc, 1dc, 1ch, 1dc, 1hdc, 1sc] in same sc as ss, remove hook, insert from back in same sc, catch loop and pull through, remove hook, insert from front in next sc, catch loop and pull through, rep from * in each sc, omitting last pull through.

Fasten off by cutting yarn and pulling end through last sc.

to finish

Weave in ends. Sew flowers on hat.

chevron bag

This bag stays firmly closed when worn but opens up easily when you take it off. When I first planned the bag, I thought I'd make it in two pieces and wrestled with trying to work out how to fill in the zigzag edges. As soon as I'd made a length of the chevron pattern, it all fell into place as I realized the bag could be made in one piece with the points making a neat finish at the top.

size
Actual measurements: width 13 in. (33 cm); length 13¼ in. (34 cm)

materials
3 x 1¾ oz. (50 g) balls of matte cotton DK in bright blue (A)
2 x 1¾ oz. (50 g) balls same in each of navy (B) and cream (C)
US 5F (4.00 mm) crochet hook
11 x 5/16 in. (8 mm) eyelet rivets
2 D rings
4½ yd (4 m) navy cord

gauge
13 sts measure 2¼ in. (5.5 cm), 12 rows to 4 in. (10 cm) over chevron patt using US 5F (4.00 mm) hook. Change hook size, if necessary, to obtain this gauge.

abbreviations
See page 17.

note
■ For neat edges, work the starting chain loosely and the last row in A tightly.

bag

Using A, make 78ch.

1st row (WS): 2sc in 2nd ch from hook, 1sc in each of next 4ch, [skip 2ch, 1sc in each of next 5ch, 3sc in foll ch, 1sc in each of next 5ch] 5 times, skip 2ch, 1sc in each of next 4ch, 2sc in last ch. 77 sts.

2nd row: 1ch, 2sc in first sc, 1sc in each of next 4sc, [skip 2sc, 1sc in each of next 5sc, 3sc in foll sc, 1sc in each of next 5sc] 5 times, skip 2sc, 1sc in each of next 4sc, 2sc in last sc.

2nd row forms chevron patt.

Work 1 more row A.

Work in stripe patt of 2 rows B, 2 rows A, 2 rows C, 2 rows A, for 76 rows, so ending with 2 rows in A.

Work 1 more row A. Fasten off.

- Carry the A yarn up the side of the work but fasten off and rejoin the B and C yarns to reduce bulk in the seams.

- The yarn used for the bag in the picture is a firm, matte cotton DK that feels almost thick enough to be an Aran weight. It has approximately 87 yards (80 meters) to a 1³/₄ oz. (50 g) ball.

- You only just break into the 2nd ball of the navy and the cream. If you made the bag with 3 contrast colors, you'd only need one ball of each.

- The chevron pattern is an ideal way of using up odd amounts of yarn. If you want to work the stripes in a random mix of colors, you'll need a total of just under 10¹/₂ oz. (300 g) of yarn.

- If you are working a random color choice but want your stripes to match at the sides, wind off half of each yarn. Use the first half ball of each color until you have worked a total of 40 rows, including the 1st row worked into the chain, then work from the 2nd half balls, reversing the color order.

to finish

Fold bag in half. Noting that the back of the bag has a half chevron at each side at the top so the front has 6 points and the back 5 points, join sides, inserting a D ring at lower edge of each side of folded edge. Set an eyelet in each chevron point. Divide cord in half. Thread one cord through the eyelets, pass one end of the cord through the D ring that's on the same side as the ends, and knot the ends loosely. Thread 2nd cord through the eyelets in the opposite direction, pass one end through the other D ring, and knot loosely. Try bag on and adjust length of cords to fit. Knot the ends firmly and trim.

This bag stays firmly closed when worn but opens up easily when you take it off

103

hipster belt

The bold motifs that make up this pretty, silky belt are worked over curtain rings to give a firm, flexible structure.

size
Actual length 36½ in. (93 cm)

materials
1 x 1¾ oz. (50 g) hank of Debbie Bliss Pure Silk in turquoise, shade 007
US C2 (2.50 mm) crochet hook
14 x ¾ in. (19 mm) curtain rings
15 x 1 in (25 mm) curtain rings
1 buckle
46 beads

gauge
When assembled, each 7-ring motif measures 4 in. (10 cm) across, each large ring motif measures 1½ in. (4 cm) across. Change hook size, if necessary, to obtain this size motifs.

abbreviations
See page 17.

note
■ For each beaded picot join, work 1sc in next sc, lengthen loop and remove hook, insert hook through a bead, catch loop, slide bead onto loop and remove hook, insert hook from the front in a picot of motif as directed, catch beaded loop and pull through picot, remove hook, insert in bead from the other end, catch loop and pull through, gauge loop tightly on hook and work 1sc in same place as last sc.

seven-ring motif
1st ring
Join yarn in a ¾ in. (19 mm) curtain ring.
1st round (RS): 1ch, 24sc in ring, ss in first sc. 24 sts **.
2nd round: 1ch, 1sc in each of first 3sc, * [1sc, 3ch, 1sc] in next sc, 1sc in each of foll 3sc, rep from * 4 more times, [1sc, 3ch, 1sc] in last sc, ss in first sc.
Fasten off.

2nd ring
As 1st ring to **.
2nd round: 1ch, 1sc in first sc, * [1sc, 3ch, 1sc] in next sc, 1sc in foll sc, rep from * 10 more times, work beaded picot join in a picot of 1st ring, ss in first sc.
Fasten off.

3rd ring
Work as 2nd ring but joining 2nd picot to 10th picot of 2nd ring and 3rd to 9th by working 1ch, ss in picot, 1ch instead of 3ch, and join last picot with a bead to next picot of 1st ring.

4th, 5th, and 6th rings
Work as 3rd ring, joining to previous ring.

7th ring
Work as 4th ring but also join 9th to 3rd and 10th to 2nd picots of 1st ring.
Make 2nd seven-ring motif in the same way.

hexagonal ring motif
1st motif
Join yarn in a 1 in. (25 mm) ring.
1st round (RS): 1ch, 30sc in ring, ss in first sc.
30 sts.
2nd round: 1ch, 1sc in each sc, ss in first sc.
3rd round: 1ch, * 1sc in each of 4sc, [1sc, 3ch, 1sc] in next sc, rep from * 3 more times, 1sc in each of next 4sc, place seven ring motif with two rings at each side and work a beaded picot join in last but one free picot of lower of the two rings at one side, 1sc in each of next 4sc, skip first free picot of adjacent upper ring,

Casual with jeans or worn with a smart dress or skirt, this belt fits the bill every time

work beaded picot join in next picot, ss in first sc.
Fasten off.

2nd motif

As 1st motif working beaded picot joins in 3rd and 2nd picots of 1st motif.

Cont making and joining hexagonal ring motifs in this way until 13 hexagonal ring motifs have been joined.

14th motif

As 2nd motif but working 2nd and 3rd picots as beaded picot joins in picots of 2nd seven-ring motif in same way as 1st ring.

15th motif

As 1st motif joining picots of 2nd seven-ring motif opposite previous join.

to finish

Cover buckle with a round of sc worked closely. Inserting beads, sew buckle to picots of 1st seven-ring motif opposite joins to 1st hexagonal ring motif. Weave in ends.

tips

- Make sure that the beads you choose have holes large enough to insert the crochet hook.

- You can easily adjust the length of the belt by joining more or less hexagonal ring motifs. Each of the motifs with the adjacent beaded join measures approximately 2 in. (5 cm). This size of curtain ring was available in packs of 12, so I bought two packs, leaving plenty of spare rings. If you are buying the rings singly, don't forget to buy more or less according to the length you want for your belt.

- Reduce the amount of ends you weave in by working over the end from the start of the 1st round when working the 2nd round.

- For a really neat join, instead of fastening off in the usual way, omit the slip stitch at the end of the last round of each motif, cut the yarn, and pull the end through the last stitch. Thread a tapestry needle with the yarn-end, take the needle under the first sc of the last round and down through the last sc to join the round before weaving in the end.

blue

armwarmers

I love the idea of something to fill the chilly gap between bare flesh and a wide coat cuff or a ¾-sleeved denim jacket. These simple tubes of textured crochet in a two-color pattern fill that space. They are worked in the round, shaped in slightly at the wrist and have holes for your thumbs.

left armwarmer

edging

Using A, make 48ch loosely, ss in first ch to form a ring.

1st round (RS): 1ch, 1sc in same place as ss, [2ch, skip 1ch, 3dctog in next ch, 2ch, skip 1ch, 1sc in next ch] 12 times, omitting last sc, ss in first sc. Fasten off.

Work in patt. With RS facing, join B in a 1ch sp along starting ch of edging.

1st round (RS): 1ch, 2sc in same 1ch sp as join, [2sc in each 1ch sp] to end, ss in first sc, turn. 48 sts.

2nd round: 1ch, [1sc in each sc] to end, change to A, ss in first sc, turn.

3rd and 4th rounds: Cont in A, work as 2nd round, changing to B at end of 4th round.

5th round: Cont in B, 1ch, 1sc in same place as ss, 2ch, 1dc in next sc, [2ch, skip 2sc, 1dc in each of next 2sc] to last 2sc, 2ch, ss in top ch, turn.

6th round: 1ch, 1sc in same place as ss, 1sc in next dc, [2ch, 1sc in each of next 2dc] to last dc, 2ch, 1sc in

last dc, change to A, ss in first sc, turn.

7th round: Cont in A, 1sc in same place as ss, 1sc in next sc, [1ddc in each of next 2sc skipped 2 rows below, 1sc in each of next 2sc] to end, omitting last 2sc, ss in first sc, turn.

8th round: 1ch, [1sc in each st] to end, change to B, ss in first sc, turn.

9th and 10th rounds: Cont in B, work as 2nd round changing to A at end of 10th round.

11th round: Cont in A, 1ch, 1sc in same place as ss, 2ch, [1dc in each sc] to end, ss in top ch, turn.

12th round: 1ch, [1sc in each dc] to end, change to B, ss in top ch, turn.

13th round: Cont in B, work as 2nd round.

2nd to 13th rounds form the patt. Patt 9 more rounds, so ending with a 10th patt round.

Dec round: Cont in A, 1sc in same place as ss, 2ch, [2dctog, 1dc in each of next 4sc] 7 times, 2dctog, 1dc in each of next 3dc, ss in top ch, turn. 40 sts.

Next round: 1ch, [1sc in each st] to

size
Actual measurements: around hand 7 in. (18 cm); length 10 in. (25 cm)

materials
1¾ oz. (50 g) of Shetland style pure wool 4ply in each of navy (A) and denim (B)
US D3 (3.00 mm) crochet hook

gauge
22 sts and 24 rows to 4 in. (10 cm) over patt using US D3 (3.00 mm) hook. Change hook size, if necessary, to obtain this gauge.

abbreviations
3dctog—leaving last loop on hook each time, work 3dc, yarn around hook and pull through 4 loops on hook.
See also page 17.

end, change to B, ss in first sc, turn. Beg 13th round, patt 22 rows, so ending with a 10th patt round **.

thumb opening

1st round (RS): Cont in A, 1sc in same place as ss, 2ch, 1dc in each of next 13sc, 6ch, skip next 6sc, 1dc in

notes

- The trebles in the 7th pattern round are worked over the 2 chain of the two previous rounds.

- When working the two-color pattern, carry yarn not in use up on WS.

- Take care to pull the slipstitch that joins each round tight so you don't mistake it for a stitch and inadvertently increase.

- You may find it easier and neater when joining a round and changing color to remove the hook before turning at the end of the round—then turn, insert hook from the front in first stitch of previous round and in last loop, catch the new color yarn and pull through.

- If you want to make a multicolor version of the armwarmers, use as many colors as you like and simply change color for each checked band and stripe in B, keeping the main color A the same throughout.

- The 4ply Shetland style wool used for these armwarmers has approximately 178 yards (163 meters) to a 1¾ oz. (50 g) ball.

each of last 20sc, ss in top ch, turn.

2nd round: 1ch, 1sc in same place as ss, 1sc in each of next 20dc, 1sc in each of next 6ch, 1sc in each of last 13dc, change to B, ss in first sc, turn.

Beg 13th round, patt 10 more rounds.

Fasten off.

thumb opening edging

Join A in first free sc in row below opening.

1st round: 1ch, 1sc in each of 6sc along lower edge of opening, 1sc in side of dc, 1sc in base of each of 6ch along upper edge of opening, 1sc in side of dc, ss in first sc, turn. 14 sts.

2nd round: 1ch, [1sc in each sc] to end, ss in first sc.

Fasten off. Weave in ends.

right armwarmer

Work as given for left armwarmer to **.

Thumb opening

1st round (RS): Cont in A, 1sc in same place as ss, 2ch, 1dc in each of next 20sc, 6ch, skip next 6sc, 1dc in each of last 13sc, ss in top ch, turn.

2nd round: 1ch, 1sc in same place as ss, 1sc in each of next 13dc, 1sc in each of next 6ch, 1sc in each of last 20dc, change to B, ss in first sc, turn.

Complete as left mitten.

Something to fill the chilly gap between bare flesh and the cropped sleeve of a denim jacket

blue

suppliers

UK

Debbie Bliss

Designer Yarns
Units 8–10
Newbridge Industrial Estate
Pitt Street, Keighley
West Yorkshire, BD21 4PQ
Tel: 01535 664222
www.designeryarns.uk.com

Sirdar and Sublime

Sirdar Spinning Ltd
Flanshaw Lane
Alverthorpe, Wakefield
West Yorkshire, WF2 9ND
Tel: 01924 371501
www.sirdar.co.uk
www.sublimeyarns.com

Colinette

Colinette Yarns
Banwy Workshops
Llanfair Caereinion
Powys, Wales
SY21 0SG
Tel: 01938 810128
Fax: 01938 810127
www.colinette.co.uk

US

Debbie Bliss, Sirdar and Sublime

Knitting Fever
315 Bayview Avenue
Amityville, NY 11701
Tel: 516 546 3600
www.knittingfever.com

index

acknowledgments

I would like to thank everyone who helped to make
this book possible.

A huge thank you to Rosemary Wilkinson for asking me to
work on this book and for her enthusiastic response to my ideas
and to Clare Sayer for seeing me through both the exciting bit, as
the items came together and the harder part of dealing with
turning the copy into a book.

Special thanks to Susie Johns for the sympathetic styling,
to the georgeous girls – Edith, Izzy, Lillie, Mary, and Roma – and to
Paul Bricknell for the lovely, lively pictures.

For creative help, I would like to thank my good friends,
Betty Speller for the Multiway Wrap and Lesley Stanfield for the
Beanie Hat, the Luxury Scarf, and the Slouchy Socks. I'd never
have made it through the projects without you!

Thank you to Susan Horan for her support and amazing
pattern checking.

For the lovely yarns which gave me so much inspiration, many
thanks to Debbie Bliss and all at Designer Yarns and to Caroline
Powell and all at Sirdar and Sublime.

Love and thanks to Peter, as always.